Millassas

MK

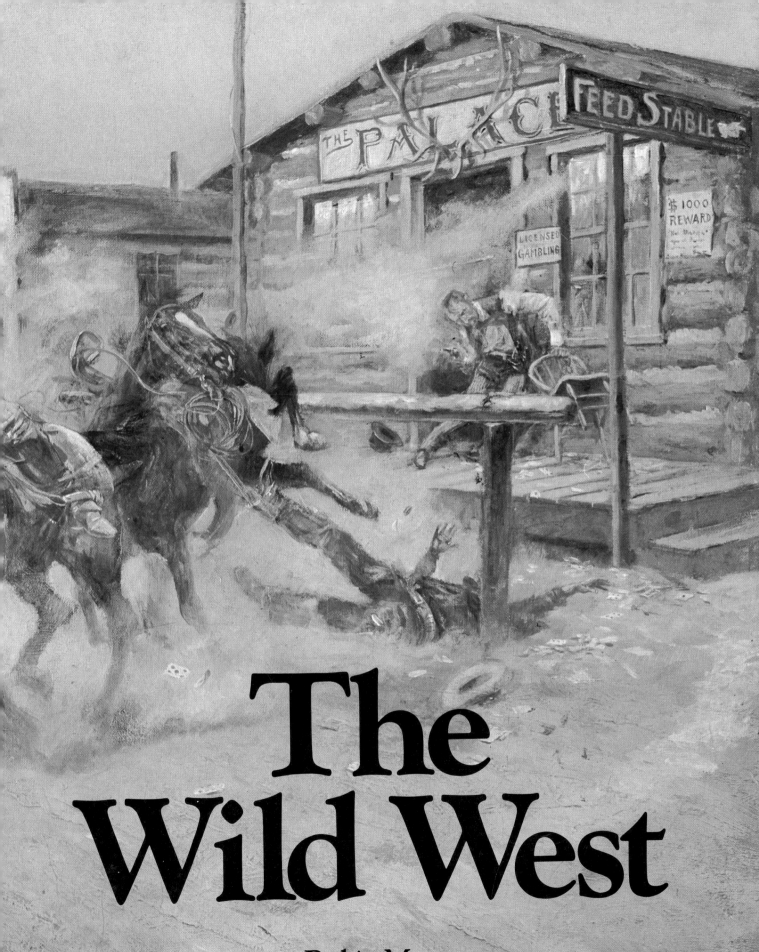

The Wild West

Robin May

First published in 1978 by
Macdonald Educational Ltd
Holywell House
Worship Street
London EC2A 2EN

© Macdonald Educational 1978

ISBN 0 356 06106 X

Printed and bound by
Purnell & Sons Ltd
Paulton
Avon
England

Contents

Before the white man came

When Columbus reached America in 1492 there were perhaps a million Indians living in what is now the United States. There were also vast herds of buffalo and an extraordinary variety of wild life, though no horses. The Indians had arrived there from Asia by crossing the narrow Bering Straits, then a land bridge, some 20,000–30,000 years ago. As to their name 'Indians', Columbus was to blame: he called them that because he was sure he had reached India, the land of spices.

Many Indians settled in what is now the West: the harsh mountains and deserts of Arizona and the Southwest; the Rocky Mountains and the Sierras of California, and the valleys between them; the thick forests of the Northwest; the high plains and the rolling prairies, the woods and lakes in the area where the River Mississippi rises.

Without horses most Indians of the West were farmers. The Sioux still lived in the forests of the Upper Mississippi from which they were later driven out by the Ojibways, but the Blackfeet were already on the plains. Some tribes lived in tents (tipis); others built earth lodges or brush huts. They moved – when they had to move – with dogs dragging their belongings on special sledges called travois. The travois were made from tent poles trailing behind the dogs with the family's belongings slung between.

The Indians hunted the buffalo which provided them with most of what they needed: food, shelter and clothing, and objects of every kind. The hunt was on foot, a slow and sometimes hazardous business. Up to 20 or 30 families would take part in the hunt, in a single band large enough to surround a small herd. Often a lot of trouble was saved by driving an entire herd of buffalo over a cliff to their death.

The Indians also fought among themselves, but without any horses this was a slow-motion affair. Sometimes it was done at long range with arrows and shields, sometimes hand to hand with lances, knives and clubs. Surprise attacks on enemy camps were usually more lethal, with women and children being captured to replace battle losses.

Indian women had a hard life, and in only a few tribes did they have any real power.

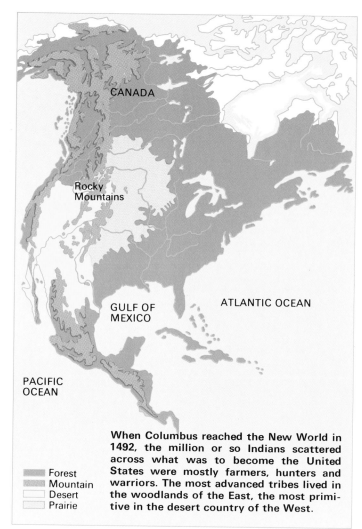

When Columbus reached the New World in 1492, the million or so Indians scattered across what was to become the United States were mostly farmers, hunters and warriors. The most advanced tribes lived in the woodlands of the East, the most primitive in the desert country of the West.

Forest
Mountain
Desert
Prairie

▲ A physical map of North America.

Indian life varied from tribe to tribe, from place to place. But some things held true for all Indians. They were deeply religious. They believed that the Earth was their mother, and were very influenced by magic. They felt a close link with the animals on whom they depended for so much. The coming of the horse, as we shall see, was to change their lives, but the white men who brought it finally destroyed the old ways and put death or despair in their place.

▶ Indian sign language. The Plains Indians consisted of many tribes, speaking different languages. Yet they could all communicate with one another thanks to the expressive sign language which was understood by Indians all over the Plains. Other peoples have used sign languages, but none as successfully as those who 'spoke' the language of the Plains.

to keep

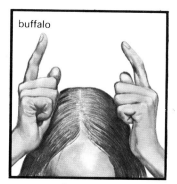

buffalo

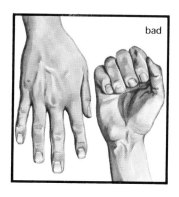

bad

An Indian family

▶ This illustration of a Blackfoot family is based on pictures painted some 150 years ago, before white influence began to change the appearance of the Plains Indians.

The Indians on the Plains had a rich family life, and children were spoiled. Women had to do most of the hard work, while men concentrated on hunting and fighting.

The tribe was all important yet individual Indians retained the right to make their own decisions. This individualism made it easier for the whites to win in the end.

The tipi in the background dates from a period when Indians had the horse. Tipis had to be smaller when dogs were used to drag the family's belongings.

▼ A painting by George Catlin showing Indians stalking buffalo. They have disguised themselves in wolves' skins in order to creep up undetected. Buffalo were not afraid of wolves.

▶ An early watercolour of Indians fishing with spears and nets, painted by John White in 1575.

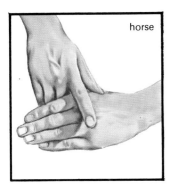
horse

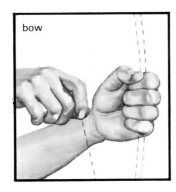
bow

dog

council

Spanish influence

Into the Southwest out of Mexico marched iron-hard men, carrying the Cross and lusting after gold. They were Spanish soldiers, led by Francisco de Coronado, and they had been lured by false reports of the Seven Cities of Cibola, said to be cities of gold. Yet why should they not believe the stories? Had not some of them seen the marvellous riches of Mexico and Peru? The year was 1540.

In fact the seven cities proved to be built of mud and stone. But although the expedition did not find gold, the Spaniards reached as far north as Kansas and cut east into Oklahoma and Texas. They were the first white men to marvel at the Grand Canyon and to see the countless buffalo herds roaming the West.

Every follower of Westerns knows something of the Spanish influence in the West, but at first it was strictly limited. Coronado's expedition was not followed up until the 1700s. A series of villages, ranches and missions were built, stretching from Florida in the east to California in the west; but it was only in California that the Spaniards had any real success. There the missions flourished as nowhere else, partly because the dedicated priests struck up excellent relations with the not very warlike Indians of the Pacific coast. Some of these Spanish buildings survive to this day.

In the Southwest, however, it was a very different story. The plains were by now filled with horses, the

▲ Spanish soldiers and an Indian foreman oversee Indians at work building a ship. The Indians were virtually slaves and there were many uprisings against their Spanish masters.

▼ In many places in California, New Mexico, Arizona and Texas which were once ruled by Spain, old Spanish missions can still be seen.

▶ Charles Russell's famous picture of a buffalo hunt is a reminder that even when the Plains Indians had learned to use horses, buffalo hunting could still be dangerous. Yet the buffalo and its by-products were essential to the survival of the tribe. Russell, a noted cowboy artist, liked and understood Indians at a time when few whites did.

Route of Coronado's expedition
Francisco Vasquez de Coronado was a young Spanish nobleman whose ability in war led to his appointment as governor of the northern Mexican province of New Galicia. Later he was chosen to lead the first expedition north into what became the American West, in search of the mythical cities of gold.

- San Francisco
- CALIFORNIA
- Santa Fé
- Independence
- TEXAS
- PACIFIC OCEAN
- MEXICO
- Compostela

descendants of those brought to the West by Coronado. The Indians had learnt to tame them, and the legendary Plains Indians came into being, marauding bands mounted on horseback, wandering at will across the prairie.

It was the southern frontier that suffered most. There, in what became Arizona, New Mexico and Texas, the dreaded Comanches carried out raid after raid on the missions. Worse still, the Apaches soon stormed on to the pages of history, feared by whites and Indians alike.

Santa Barbara, 1833
The Spanish mission of Santa Barbara was started in 1786 and completed in 1833. It was one of a number of missions built by Franciscan friars.

church

workshops

patio

priest's quarters

storerooms

Missions were miniature towns run by the Fathers and Christian Indians. Note the church, the priest's quarters in the right foreground, and the wide patios.

As well as being a church and a centre for conversion, most missions were trading posts. They also farmed the land around.

The last Spanish hold on the West was lost in 1821, when Mexico broke away from Spanish rule. Yet this did not prevent the influence of Spain from remaining strong in the United States. It can still be seen in place names such as Los Angeles and San Francisco, in some fine old architecture, in words like 'rancho' and 'rodeo', and even in the clothes the cowboys like to wear. Today there are many thousand Mexican Americans living in the USA, despite the fact that Mexico finally lost California to the USA in 1848. And it is to Spain that America owes its orange and lemon trees.

Yet it was the animals the Spaniards introduced to the West which have left the most mark.

The coming of the horse revolutionized the Indians' traditional way of life, banishing the dog days for ever and transforming even those who had been farmers into nomads and warriors.

The Spaniards also introduced cattle and, as we shall see (pages 28–29), it was their descendants that became the hard-hided, history-making longhorns. They in turn gave rise to the American cowboy, who remains one of the key figures in the real Wild West.

Lewis and Clark

The great adventure began with the most magnificent land deal in history. In 1803, President Jefferson of the USA brought from France the entire Mississippi Valley westwards to the Rocky Mountains for only 15 million dollars. The sellers knew almost nothing about the area they called Louisiana, which was much vaster than the present state of that name. Only a handful of explorers had been there. Now it was the Americans' turn.

Jefferson sent an expedition into the 'Louisiana Purchase' territory to try and find a water route to the Pacific. The leaders, Captain Meriwether Lewis and Lieutenant William Clark, were also told to study the Indian tribes they encountered and the flora and fauna along the route.

They started up the River Missouri in May 1804, and spent the winter at what is now Bismarck, North Dakota, with the Mandan Indians. The following spring, the party of 32 set off again and, miraculously, all survived their epic journey. It helped that they, un-like later Americans, befriended the Indians they met. It also helped that Lewis and Clark had hired a French-Canadian trapper, whose wife was a young Shoshone girl named Sacajawea. She helped to guide the party and acted as an interpreter. Sacajawea had a baby that she carried on her back, and the sight of them helped convince Indian tribes that the party was peaceful.

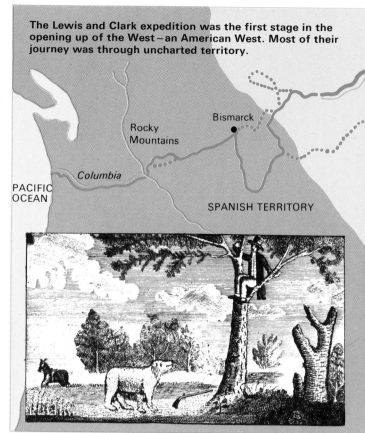

The Lewis and Clark expedition was the first stage in the opening up of the West—an American West. Most of their journey was through uncharted territory.

Rocky Mountains

Bismarck

Columbia

PACIFIC OCEAN

SPANISH TERRITORY

Meriwether Lewis

The woodcuts on this page appeared in the first pub-lished account of the Lewis and Clark expedition. The shaggy creature above is supposed to be a grizzly bear. Top right shows Lewis and Clark parleying with an Indian chief. The picture on the right illustrates an unfortunate accident!

▼ A keelboat, the main type of craft used by the expedition.

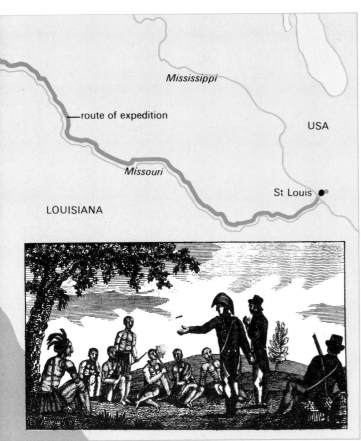

As well as the Indian Sacajawea and her baby, the party included a black man, Clark's slave York, who was later freed by his master. He thoroughly enjoyed his trip, not least because the Indian maidens greatly admired him! Lewis also took his big Northumberland dog along. Scannon was his name and the Indians admired him, too.

In November 1805 the expedition reached the mouth of the Columbia River. They had found no direct water route to the Pacific and now spent an uncomfortable winter in a makeshift fort. Cold, rainy weather at last gave way to spring and they set out for home. The party split in two in order to cover more ground, and reached St Louis in September 1806.

The expedition was a peaceful start to many years of bloodshed in the West. Lewis and Clark diligently collected masses of information about the unknown land which was now part of their country. Their journals, which appeared in print some years later, are classics of exploration.

As for Lewis and Clark themselves, the former became Governor of Louisiana Territory, but died in mysterious circumstances in Tennessee, either killing himself, for he had become a moody man, or being murdered. Clark was first made Governor of Missouri, then Superintendent of Indians, and he arranged to have Sacajawea's three children well educated.

leatherbound journal

peace medal

◄ Two of the items Lewis and Clark took with them on their expedition. They had been ordered to find out as much as possible about the territory through which they were passing and the Indians they met, and they kept a comprehensive journal about their journey. They also took a special peace medal to give to Indian tribes.

William Clark

The mountain men

Their business was beaver and they were the most rugged men who ever explored the West. Beaver fur was high fashion in the early 19th century, between 1810 and the 1830s, and there were men daring enough to take any risk to obtain the valuable fur.

Though they were called 'Mountain Men', the trappers crossed deserts and plains as well, and, incidentally, blazed trails right across the West that later travellers used. They were loners by nature, living like the Indians and in the process getting to know Indians as few whites ever had.

Some of the mountain men are legends to this day: Jim Bridger and Kit Carson, and Jedediah Smith, who pioneered the trail to California before perishing by a Comanche lance. Another was John Colter, who had travelled with Lewis and Clark. He was captured by the Blackfeet who stripped him, gave him a head start and then pursued him, brandishing spears. Colter, his bare feet torn by thorns and rocks, reached the Madison River nine kilometres away, having managed to trip up and kill the only Indian to get near him. He hid under driftwood while the furious Blackfeet roamed the bank. When they gave up the chase he swam down river and started on a 300-kilometre trek towards his base camp. He arrived starving and bloodstained, a ghastly apparition, but being a true mountain man he soon recovered.

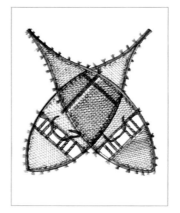

▲ Snowshoes, an essential part of any mountain man's equipment, particularly in winter time.

▲ Typical beaver traps as used by mountain men. The design changed little over the years.

▶ A mountain man

The mountain man had to be prepared to fight Indians and grizzly bears, and to survive in deserts, snows and every sort of wilderness in his quest for beaver fur.

He lived and worked before the days of repeating rifles. Although his rifle, often a Hawken, was very powerful, it took so long to load that Indians had more than a sporting chance against him: they could shoot far more arrows than he could bullets. More than anyone else, these dauntless trappers blazed trails across the West, finding salt lakes and hot geysers, and being dubbed liars for their pains.

They were experts with knives and pistols as well as rifles, and were as much at home in the wilderness as any wild animal – or Indian. Most of them were white Americans, but there were black mountain men too, and some French Canadians and Britons. Many of them started life on farms, but few of them returned to farming when the fur trade collapsed.

◄ After eleven months of hard work, the mountain man had one glorious month on the spree at a rendezvous camp, drinking, trading, horseracing, gambling, fighting, boasting and even sometimes finding a bride. Then, with the beaver furs sold and all the money gone, it was back to the mountains for another year.

The big event in the mountain man's year was the annual rendezvous camp, held every summer. Fur companies sent their agents to the camps, who brought with them goods, weapons, tools and hard cash to exchange for furs of all sorts, but particularly for beaver. Often a mountain man would gamble away all his money in a single night. The camp was a riotous spot: horse-racing, fighting and drinking by day, and gambling and raucous laughter by night. Here, too, a trapper might acquire for himself an Indian bride.

By the 1840s, however, beaver fur had gone out of fashion and the fur trade collapsed. The mountain men, those that were still alive, turned instead to scouting, or guiding explorers and wagon trains on the trail West. Only very rarely did they take up farming or head eastwards to the big cities. These hardy early Americans had seen the Old West in all its beauty and grandeur; their lives made characters like Jesse James and Wild Bill Hickok seem tame by comparison; and they were not the settling kind.

◄ Beaver skins were widely used in hat-making until the 1840s. This watercolour shows a New York warehouse displaying 'fashionable Beaver hats'. This is where the fur obtained by the mountain men ended up!

▼ The hard-working, skilful beaver was the object of a mountain man's existence. Its cleverly built home could not save it from the trappers, however, and in the end beaver became almost extinct in the American West.

The beavers lived on twigs and bark from the frail aspen. They needed a water-sealed entrance-exit to give them privacy. But this was little protection for them against determined mountain men.

15

Trails west

Ever since pioneers had crossed the Appalachian Mountains in the 1770s, when the American Revolution was still raging, and staked a claim to Indian land in the first West, there had been a steady movement westwards by men, women and children. What drove them west? The lure of new lands, the promise of better ones, the feeling of being hemmed in, sheer wanderlust: all these were factors. But there was nothing in American history to equal the great migrations of the 1840s, 'across the Wide Missouri' to Oregon and California.

The first great trail, the Santa Fé, was in use by the 1820s, but it was a trading trail, not a pioneer route. The history-making Oregon fever hit the USA in the early 1840s, when American patriotism was added to the lure of land. The British Hudson's Bay Company had laid claim to the great Northwest, and the American government in retaliation offered land in Oregon to anyone who would go there, so that it could claim the area was occupied by American settlers and therefore rightfully part of America. The few who had made the journey came back with glowing reports of the Promised Land they had found there, and found willing listeners among their friends and neighbours, eager for adventure, or for a new start in life.

The great 3,000-kilometre trek started just beyond Independence, Missouri. The California Trail branched off from the Oregon Trail at Fort Hall, but this only became important after the Californian gold strikes of 1848. It was really the Oregon Trail, heading out into the unknown territory of Oregon, that has come down through history as the great pioneer trail.

Ten thousand men, women and children braved the plains and mountains to reach the Promised Land of Oregon. They were true heroes. They gained the Northwest for their nation and put down roots that stuck. Indeed the pioneers, though not as 'romantic' as the cowboys and Indians, were the supreme white heroes of the Western story, risking death on their journey and surviving the hardships – which were especially hard on women – in a new land. They had just their bare hands, and the few tools they could take with them, to help them carve out a new life for themselves.

There was one movement westwards like no other. The Mormons were a religious sect uninterested in gold or adventure, wanting only the religious freedom they were denied in the East. The sect had been founded in 1830 in New York by Joseph Smith, but it was the inspiration of Brigham Young which saved it after persecution broke out, caused partly by Smith's proclamation that a man could have more than one wife. Smith was murdered, but Brigham Young led his people to the Salt Lake Valley of Utah, where the Mormons 'made the desert bloom' and built Salt Lake City.

▲ The interior of old Fort Laramie in Wyoming, a key point on the Oregon Trail, where pioneers had a chance to rest and recover for the next stage of their journey. Fort Laramie began as a fur-trade centre. In later years it was a major military outpost during the Indian Wars.

▼ Pulling or pushing their handcarts, some 3,000 Mormons marched across the Plains to the Promised Land – Salt Lake City – covering 50 kilometres a day. They did not seek gold or adventure or vast tracts of land, just a place to practise their faith.

The Mormon trail was made more remarkable by the fact that the converts, coming from all over the world, used handcarts in which to pull their belongings across the rugged country. More than 3,000 Mormons travelled in this way, averaging 50 kilometres a day, which was more than twice as fast as the rate over the Oregon Trail.

The great trails west

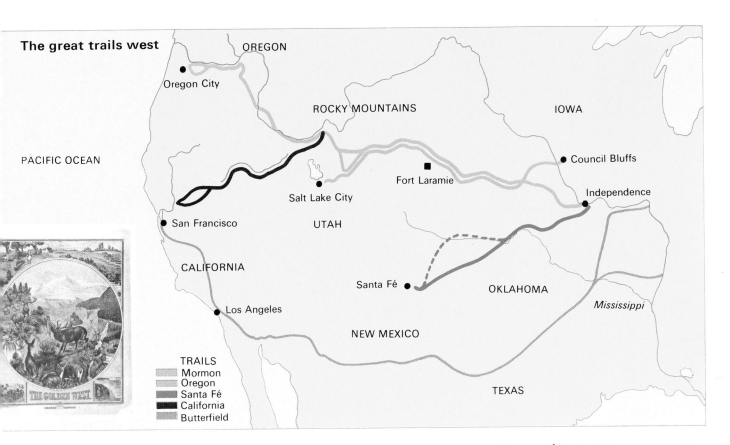

TRAILS
- Mormon
- Oregon
- Santa Fé
- California
- Butterfield

▲ The great trails West. The earliest was the Santa Fé, which was used mainly for trade. The Oregon Trail was the most famous; it secured the Northwest for the USA. The California Trail came into its own after gold was found near San Francisco. The Mormon Trail was for some a road to religious freedom.

◄ Each night wagons on the Oregon Trail went into a circle for protection against Indian attack. Yet the Indians did not attack an Oregon train in the 1840s. The attacks only came later, when the Indians began to fear they would lose all their lands.

▼ Many of the first settlers' houses were built just out of sods of earth.

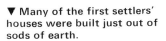

▼ A proud family of settlers photographed outside their new home in Nebraska.

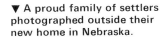

The pioneers

Westward the wagons! Every spring from the early 1840s onwards the pioneers set out, hoping to reach Oregon before winter. A wagon trail was like a creaking town on wheels, with hundreds of families and men of every trade, including a fair share of gamblers and killers. Many rode in converted farm wagons, covered in canvas and with buckets hanging underneath. All their equipment and the goods they would need were stored inside. There was little room for luxuries.

At first the going was easy, through the meadows and gentle hills of eastern Kansas. Oxen were soon found to be better trail animals than horses or mules. The first mass crossing, the 'Great Emigration' of 1843, had a pilot to lead it plus a Captain and a Council of Ten. Like later expeditions this one found the river crossings hard going. The Platte River in particular, with its many quicksands, took nearly a week to cross. In 1843 they made rafts from the tops of their wagons.

The train was kept in line in the river by a chain.

On the great expanse of the central Plains later travellers sometimes found the shallow graves of earlier pioneers, or possessions from over-burdened wagons and the carcasses of horses and oxen. Sickness and disease were a constant threat. Huge herds of buffalo could also hold up the trail, but at least dried buffalo dung provided them with fuel. Babies suffered continually from nappy rash and not until Fort Laramie was reached could anyone wash their clothes.

Wagon trains aimed to cover 15 kilometres a day. Oregon and California had to be reached before the snows settled deep. One unhappy party that failed to get to California on time and was trapped by the snow resorted to cannibalism. The last stage of the journey, through the Rocky Mountains, was the most dangerous. On the Devil's Backbone wagons crawled along a ridge $1\frac{1}{2}$ kilometres long with a 300-metre gorge on one side and a sheer slope on the other.

▼ A sturdy Prairie Schooner, of the type used to carry thousands of families westwards to Oregon. A wagon like this would spell home to many thousands of ordinary people bound for a new start and a new life in the West.

The wagon bed, a rectangular wooden box, was literally the only resting place they had for months on end. It was just over a metre wide and nearly four metres long. In front of it was the jockey box which carried the tools.

There were iron tyres on the wheels and hanging from the rear axle was a grease bucket for lubricating the wheels. A hickory wood frame supported the canvas cover of the wagon, which was their only protection against the weather.

There was little comfort for the travellers, though in really hot weather the cover could be folded back. The wagon had no springs, and so much cargo was loaded aboard that it was sometimes hard to find space to sit down.

Many early pioneers took to the foaming rivers rather than risk falling to their death. From the safety of his own boat a boy named Jesse Applegate saw disaster overtake some of his family on the Columbia River: 'The boat we were watching disappeared and we saw the men and boys struggling in the water. Father and Uncle Jesse, seeing their children drowning, were seized with frenzy, and dropping their oars, sprang up from their seats and were about to leap from the boat to make a desperate attempt to swim to them.' Jesse's mother and his Aunt Cynthia stopped them from committing suicide in the raging torrent in which both his cousins were drowned. Other pioneers perished trying to take short cuts across the harsh desert. But the majority survived to put down roots in their new land.

Meanwhile, back in Independence, Missouri, wagons were already being prepared for the next crossing. America was on the move.

▼ Some of the items carried on their journey by the early pioneers. They had to take everything they needed with them, for there were no shops where they were going. Often the pioneers did not know what conditions they would meet. Space was limited in the wagon and packing had to be done with care. Most pioneers took a mixture of essential items, tools, medical aids, weapons, clothing and blankets, even seeds; and a few luxuries, such as perhaps some fine linen or silverware.

▲ A perfectly restored pioneer wagon crossing the prairie. How would you like to spend three months cooped up in one of these?

◄ Indian attack.
The flood of whites who began crossing the Plains in the 1850s caused fear among the Indians, who started to attack the wagon trains. When attacked by Indians the wagons usually formed into a defensive circle, known as a 'corral'. This was very difficult to penetrate, even by charging Indians on horseback.

shotgun

axe

ox yoke

skillet

coffee grinder

wagon jack

tar bucket

medical kit

blanket

lantern

Remember the Alamo!

Texans have never been shy about proclaiming the glories, past and present, of their native state, not least the truly glorious story of the Alamo.

American settlers began flooding into Texas in the 1820s. At that time it was still part of Mexico, newly independent of Spain. From the start the newcomers and their Mexican rulers were uneasy neighbours. In the mid-1830s the Americans rebelled against the new ruler of Mexico, President Santa Anna. The overall advantage of numbers lay with the rebels, for there were now 30,000 Americans in Texas and only 7,000 Mexicans. Undeterred, an enraged Santa Anna headed northwards with a small army to punish the arrogant interlopers and their newly elected leader, Sam Houston.

The Mexicans quickly closed in on the Alamo, once a mission and now a fortress located at San Antonio. Defended by some 180, it was to hold out against an army of 4,000 from 23 February to 6 March, 1836.

Inside the Alamo itself there were three commanders: Davy Crockett, a frontiersman and politician who was already a legend; Jim Bowie, a landowner and duellist who had given his name to a famous knife; and, nominally their superior, a hot-tempered lawyer, William Travis.

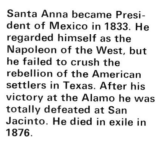

Santa Anna became President of Mexico in 1833. He regarded himself as the Napoleon of the West, but he failed to crush the rebellion of the American settlers in Texas. After his victory at the Alamo he was totally defeated at San Jacinto. He died in exile in 1876.

Samuel Houston was a larger than life character. After being Governor of Tennessee, he spent three years with the Cherokee Indians before leading Texas in its revolt against Mexico. He was the first President of an independent Texas, and today is the supreme hero of all Texans.

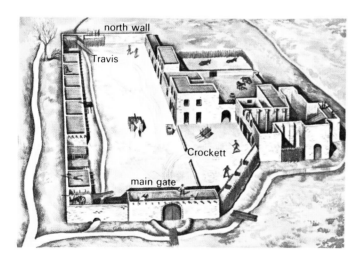

▲ A plan of the Alamo fort at the time of the battle. The defenders were brave, but they could only hold out for a day against the vastly superior numbers of the Mexicans who surrounded the fort. The north wall was breached, and then it was only a matter of time . . .

◀ The best-known version of the famous Bowie knife. It was an alarming weapon in the right hands – for stabbing, chopping or slicing!

Jim Bowie was a legend long before he died at the Alamo. He was a renowned knife fighter and he invented – or, at least, popularized – the deadly Bowie knife illustrated here (bottom left). He was also a crack pistol shot and a shrewd businessman. His family died shortly before him.

Davy Crockett remains a Frontier immortal. He was a mighty hunter, a mighty orator and a mighty liar, a politician as well as a fighter. Like Sam Houston, he came from Tennessee, and he died a hero's death at the Alamo. He was 49 when he was killed fighting for Texas.

Travis sent a message to the people of Texas and all Americans, asking for help, and ending with the stirring words, 'Victory or Death'. When he heard that no help was forthcoming, he assembled his men, and told them that anyone who wished to could escape. Those who wanted to stay and fight were to cross a line he proceeded to draw in the dirt on the ground. All crossed the line except one man; even Jim Bowie, desperately ill, was carried across. The one man, Moses Rose, escaped to tell the tale, which, as it did him no credit, was probably true.

The remaining heroes died, along with hundreds of their enemies. Out of the holocaust a mere 15 women and children survived. But the dead had given Sam Houston time to build up his forces. That April, Santa Anna, by now dangerously over-confident, was surprised by the Texans at San Jacinto. In a 20-minute battle he was utterly routed. The Texans shouted 'Remember the Alamo!' as they fought – to such good effect that 600 Mexicans were killed, and only nine Texans.

So Texas gained independence as a sovereign nation. In 1847, it finally became part of the United States, as Sam Houston had always wanted. The gallant defenders of the Alamo had not died in vain.

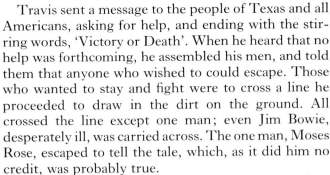

◄ Davy Crockett's last stand at the Alamo. No one knows for certain the details of the last moments of the battle, so the illustration is inevitably partly imaginary. One thing is certain; the defenders died hard, and both sides suffered terrible casualties.

▲ The Alamo at San Antonio in Texas is today preserved as a national monument. The former mission fortress, now a museum, is known as 'the cradle of Texas liberty'. It looks quite peaceful in the sunshine, and it is hard to imagine that a bloody battle once surged around it.

Gold rush

Gold fever swept whole continents in the 19th century. News of a strike, or even a rumour of one, caused an immediate stampede. Ships in the ports nearby were abandoned by their crews, while other ships set sail from countries far away, carrying thousands of passengers caught up in the same golden dream.

Many never arrived at the goldfields and many more never found any gold, but a few found wealth beyond their wildest hopes. The most important strike of the century happened in California in 1848. A man named James Marshall found gold near a sawmill belonging to John Sutter on the American River. The pair tried to keep the news a secret among Sutter's employees, but they failed: someone brandished a bottle containing gold dust in the tiny village of San Francisco, and the rush was on. Soon San Francisco was anything but tiny.

At first the rush was a local affair, as almost the entire population of the area joined in a frantic race for the hills. One Californian later recalled how 'all were off to the mines, some on carts, some on horses, some on crutches, and one went in a litter'.

As the news spread prospectors came from far and wide to search for the magic gold metal. Some risked their lives cutting across the fever-ridden Isthmus of Panama (where the canal now runs); others risked Indian arrows, starvation and thirst crossing the Plains westwards and scaling mountain ranges to reach the gold fields. The men of 1849 – the immortal 'Forty-Niners' – were on their way.

California's white population soared from 20,000 to 250,000 in four years. In 1852, 81 million dollars' worth of gold was found, and by 1900 more than 1,000 million dollars' worth had been extracted from the Californian mines.

Yet only a few prospectors became rich. Finding gold was always a matter of luck. Many never uncovered even a single particle of dust. Many others were robbed of their finds or killed. There was little law and order in the gold towns, and miners often banded together to take the law into their own hands. The men who prospered most were the merchants and financiers who made large profits out of gold and sold goods to the miners at often extortionate prices. And not only California, the Golden State, prospered: so did the nation, as the money created by the gold was put to use.

Soon there were finds elsewhere, in Nevada and Montana, Colorado and Arizona. The century ended with the Klondike stampede of 1898 after gold had been found in a remote region of Canada, near the Alaskan border. Over 30,000 managed to reach the Klondike, the last of the great gold rushes. Mining today in the West's few remaining mines is highly technical, but some prospectors continue to dream of a lucky strike. The lure of gold seems eternal.

'A gold hunter on his way to California'.

A teasing look at the Forty-Niners and the gear they took with them to California. Note the veritable arsenal that our hero is carrying in his pocket. Note also the string of sausages, for sustenance, and the essential mining equipment – right down to the tea-pot!

◀ Early photographs taken during the Californian gold rush. Note the woman bringing a picnic lunch to her menfolk (far left), and the Chinese coolies (left). Thousands of Chinese came to California seeking gold and were often persecuted for being 'different'.

▼ A view of San Francisco as it was at the very start of the gold rush. The men are milling around the post office, perhaps wanting to lay claim to their stake, or calling for friends and relatives to join them in this truly 'golden' land.

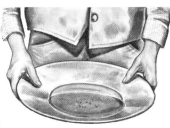

Swirling the dirt round in the pan to separate the gold.

Pouring off the water. Any gold would remain in the pan.

Ways of finding gold
◀ The classic method of extracting gold was by panning. A miner swirled 'pay dirt', earth thought to contain gold, round and round in a flat pan filled with water. Every so often he poured off the water, and with it the light dirt. The gold, being heavier, stayed at the bottom of the pan.

▶ A less tiring method of finding gold was the cradle, a wooden box on rockers. Into this was fitted a canvas covered 'apron', and on top of that a hopper with a handle to move the cradle from side to side. The dirt was piled on the hopper with its perforated base. Water was then poured on top. When it ran out, any gold-bearing sediment was caught on the riffles.

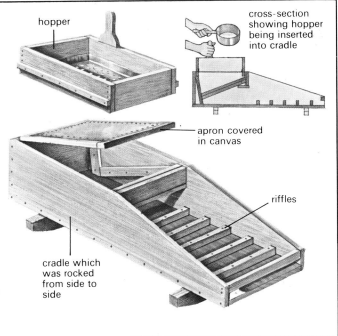

hopper

cross-section showing hopper being inserted into cradle

apron covered in canvas

riffles

cradle which was rocked from side to side

Frontier towns

A 'town' in the old West could be anything from a booming frontier community, complete with schools, churches, stores and some less reputable institutions, to a handful of shacks perched on the 'lone prairie'. Some of the first American towns west of the Missouri River were erected in Oregon in the 1840s at the end of the Oregon Trail.

When gold was discovered in California, 'towns' quickly sprang up in the mountains and valleys. Their features at first included an almost total lack of women, even dance-hall girls. The plainest lady was stared at in open-mouthed admiration, and at dances men danced with men. The first gold rush towns were tent or shack villages, hurriedly erected with whatever materials came to hand. Very soon, however, some towns such as San Francisco, and Sacramento, the state capital, rapidly became the genuine article, with proper laid-out streets, and a form of town planning.

The most notorious Western towns were the cow-towns of Kansas, where Texas cowboys congregated to celebrate in the bars. Even wilder were the 'end of track' towns erected on a temporary basis while a particular stretch of railroad was being built. Lawmen had to be very tough to cope with the riotous living of hundreds of men who laid the track by day, and by night enjoyed the basic pleasures offered by the sharks of both sexes who followed them. Rotgut liquor hardly helped to cool tempers, and fierce fights were frequent. Most of the tent towns vanished as the rails moved on, or rather, were packed up and moved on as well; a few, notably Cheyenne in Wyoming, turned gradually into stable communities.

Some towns were fairly respectable from the start, though few were as God-fearing as the Mormons' Salt Lake City. Some, like Abilene, gained almost instant respectability by banishing the cattle trade, a brave step since it meant depriving the town of the cattlemen's money.

There was one remarkable case of a major town built in a single day. This was Guthrie in Oklahoma Territory, which grew from a population of nil to 10,000 in the course of one afternoon in April 1889. The government declared some Indian land open territory; on the great day 60,000 men, women and children crossed the border from Kansas to lay claim to their portion. Many were furious to discover that 300 people had jumped the gun and come in a day early. They were nicknamed 'sooners', which was later adopted as a motto by all Oklahomans, even the 'laters'.

▲ An early photograph of Nevada City. Its construction looks rather rocky!

◄ A Kansas general store, showing both goods and customers.

▼ Ladies were a rare sight in early Western towns.

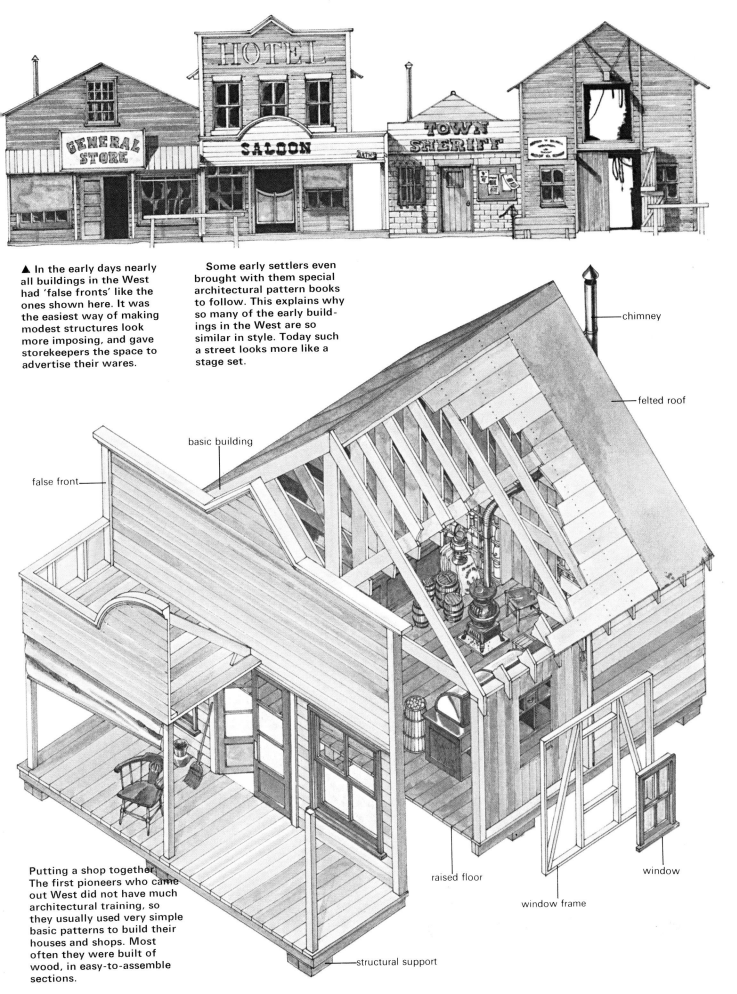

▲ In the early days nearly all buildings in the West had 'false fronts' like the ones shown here. It was the easiest way of making modest structures look more imposing, and gave storekeepers the space to advertise their wares.

Some early settlers even brought with them special architectural pattern books to follow. This explains why so many of the early buildings in the West are so similar in style. Today such a street looks more like a stage set.

chimney

felted roof

basic building

false front

window

window frame

raised floor

structural support

Putting a shop together. The first pioneers who came out West did not have much architectural training, so they usually used very simple basic patterns to build their houses and shops. Most often they were built of wood, in easy-to-assemble sections.

Conmen and showmen

BUFFALO BILL'S WILD WEST
AND CONGRESS OF ROUGH RIDERS OF THE WORLD.

COL.W.F.CODY
"BUFFALO BILL"
WILL APPEAR
AT EVERY PERFORMANCE

A COMPANY OF WILD WEST COWBOYS. THE REAL ROUGH RIDERS OF THE WORLD WHOSE DARING EXPLOIT HAVE MADE THEIR VERY NAMES SYNONYMOUS WITH DEEDS OF BRAVER

The West was wide open territory for swarms of conmen – and women – eager to extract every possible cent from gullible dudes, suckers, cowboys, travellers, and indeed anyone else who fell into their clutches.

Some of these confidence tricksters were crooked gamblers at a time when it was considered respectable for even a lawman to spend much of his time at the card tables. One Wyoming lawman combined his job of maintaining order with that of saloon-keeper; later it was found he was robbing his clients after first having drugged them.

Meanwhile, from the 1860s onwards, patent medicine men invaded the West, selling alleged elixirs guaranteed to cure everything from lumbago to baldness. Hamlin's Wizard Oil, Blood Pills and Cough Balsam were sent out from Chicago by the gallon each year, complete with a male voice quartet to lure the customers on, while one 'painless' dentist employed a band to drown the cries of his unhappy victims.

The most notorious conman – in Colorado and during the 1898 Klondike gold rush – was Jefferson 'Soapy' Smith, who had a fine voice, looked eminently respectable, and made a fortune selling sticks

of shaving soap to 'suckers' who believed that they contained dollar bills. He sold five-dollar sticks, and would wrap the sticks up in front of the miners, making sure that they saw a note go into one of them. As it was usually a 100-dollar bill, the miners quickly rushed to buy the rest. But almost all the other sticks were just – soap.

At Skagway, one of the American gateways to the Klondike, Soapy went further, and took over the entire town. He and his gang of crooks ran the theatres and dance halls, and also the carriers who took baggage to the top of the passes into the Klondike. Few prospectors managed to get through Skagway unscathed. In the end the town rose against Soapy and his gang, and the distinguished-looking 'King of the Conmen' was shot.

A happier side of the Western scene were the thriving shows, plays and musical entertainments, many of high quality. The West also exported its own brand of entertainment, the most famous example being Buffalo Bill's Wild West Show. This daring scout and buffalo hunter switched to show business with colossal success, far outstripping the rivals who tried to copy him.

◄ A poster for Buffalo Bill's famous Wild West Show. Like many Westerners, Buffalo Bill Cody told tall stories, yet his career before becoming a showman – as a Pony Express rider, hunter and Indian fighter – was genuinely exciting. He was one of the few Westerners of his day who got on well with Indians; they flocked to join his show.

► Gambling was rife in the West, where there was not much amusement, and there were plenty of 'suckers' eager to try their hand against the professionals. This crowd are playing faro. Playing against the bank at faro was known as 'bucking the tiger'.

▲ 'A Mis-deal', by Remington, shows what could happen when a trigger-happy gambler thought he was being cheated by his cronies.

► Patent medicines in fancy containers were popular all over the West. They were guaranteed to cure just about every known ailment, and some unknown ones as well! Most of them were harmless, if sometimes rather over-priced.

Indians, often straight from the warpath, joined him, as did trick riders and the fabulous 'lady shootist', Annie Oakley. Buffalo Bill even brought some of the braves who had helped to wipe out Custer on his tours to Britain and Europe. His 1887 trip, which included a long season in London, was perhaps the most successful overseas show ever seen in Britain, and was enjoyed by Queen Victoria herself. The master showman later gave four kings and the Prince of Wales a ride in a genuine Deadwood stage!

Cowboy on the ranch

The American cowboy! Today he seems a character from a legend: with the Plains Indian and the gunfighter, he is one of the great symbolic figures of the Wild West. Yet a true cowboy would probably laugh if he knew this – for he was in reality a tough, working man, who rolled out of his bunk or his bedroll around 4 in the morning and as soon as possible mounted his horse. He hated walking almost as much as he loathed sheepmen, whose animals, he alleged, cropped bare the grass and ruined every waterhole. No true cowboy would ever dream of eating mutton, or being seen in the company of sheepmen.

The Texas cattle industry began in the 1830s, at the time when Texas was breaking away from Mexico. The Texans laid claim to all the cattle they could muster. Mostly they were hard-hided longhorns, descendants of the cattle the Spaniards had brought to the New World. The Texans started ranching, and then drove the herds north and east, where there were already cowboys on a smaller scale.

The grass was good in Texas, and it was ideal cattle country. Then in 1861 came the Civil War, and when it was over in 1865 the defeated Texans returned home to find most of their ranches run down, and hundreds of thousands of longhorns running wild. The cattle ranchers and their men worked hard to build up what was to become a boom industry, especially after the herd trail north began again in the late 1860s on a far larger scale than before (see pages 30–31).

Meanwhile there was plenty to do on the ranch. The spring and autumn round-ups were the most important events, but there was much routine work: branding, breaking horses (though expert bronco busters usually did this), mending fences, looking for strays, fighting prairie fires, even pulling longhorns out of bogs.

Relaxation was hard to come by. Most ranchers forbade drinking and some banned card-playing because of the quarrels they caused. Dances were popular, but cowboys often had to dance with each other. Singing was also enjoyed. Contrary to legend, however, this was not done within earshot of the cattle, except perhaps a very soft singing as a cowboy approached his charges. The highly-strung longhorns were liable to stampede at any sudden sound, and the popular image of the cowboy singing as he went about his work is almost certainly not correct.

Some people criticise cowboys (also known as drovers) because of their intolerance of outsiders – notably Indians, Mexicans, settlers, townsmen, and of course sheepmen, whom they sometimes killed along with the sheep. But cowboys were loyal to their bosses and to one another, and tried never to harm a woman or child. And if they let off steam too energetically from time to time, this was hardly surprising. They led lonely, hard-working, sometimes dangerous lives.

A typical ranch.

lariat

branding irons

A trail boss

Inside the ranch house.

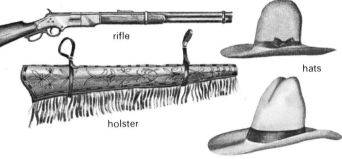

rifle

holster

hats

▲ Some of the equipment a cowboy had to be able to use: (far left) a lariat, and branding irons; (above) a Winchester rifle and holster. The hat was essential gear in the hot Texas sun.

◄ A tough-looking trail boss, armed with rifle and pistol, and a pair of cased binoculars. His lariat (lasso rope) hangs from his saddle and he is wearing chaps to protect his legs. The bandana round his neck would keep the sun off, keep dust from his nose and mouth, even serve as a towel or a bandage.

The cowboy's gear looks all American, but much of it stemmed from the clothing and equipment used by Mexican cowboys, known as *vaqueros*. The typical broad-brimmed hats, however, were much smaller than those worn by the Mexicans, who also went in for brighter colours.

Cowboys had a hard life and their work at home on the ranch – as opposed to on the trail – was often boring.

Roping a cow

Cowboys had to be expert in handling a rope, for it was usually their only means of catching an awkward or run-away cow, or one that they wanted to brand. The series of illustrations above show the most common way of roping a cow. Most often two cowboys worked together as a team. One cowboy roped the head, and his mate then made a heel catch, sliding the rope under the animal's hind legs. The heel catch was tightened and the animal was then caught. If they wanted to brand him the two riders would slowly separate so that the cow was forced down onto the ground between them. Other cow-hands would then move in for the branding.

Cowboy on the trail

The market for cattle was a poor one in Texas after the Civil War, but exciting rumours came from the north of steers selling at 50 dollars a head. A visionary named Joseph McCoy, a cattle dealer by profession, decided to take advantage of this and swing the cattle trade north to Chicago, instead of east to St Louis, Missouri, its previous headquarters. He directed his cattlemen to a spot on the new railroad called Abilene, then just a collection of huts. After the first herds had been up the trail in 1867, Abilene became the first great cowtown. The trail was named the Chisholm, after a half-Indian, half-Scot named Jesse Chisholm who had blazed it, and by 1871, 600,000 longhorns had gone up it to the markets in the north.

The great drives out of Texas usually took four months. They were run on almost military lines by rugged trail bosses, who tried to keep a steady pace of 20 kilometres a day. The trail boss led the way, with drag men at the rear to cut off stragglers and help weaklings. Baggage was carried in the chuck wagons along with beans, molasses and other supplies.

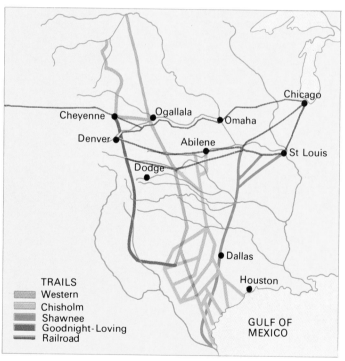

▲ Like a great snake, a herd of longhorns winds its way northwards in this painting, 'The Trail Drive', by Koerner. Apart from their dangerous horns, longhorns were renowned for their toughness and endurance. One Westerner claimed that he would prefer to meet a wounded bear in all its fierceness to a wounded longhorn bull. But the cowboy on horseback knew how to handle them.

▶ The chuck wagon was introduced to the West by Charles Goodnight in 1866. He developed it from an ordinary wagon, adding the chuck box with its hinged table and drawers for food. The cook managed the chuck wagon and was regarded as the key man in an outfit, especially on the trail. He ranked directly under the trail boss and was paid more than the cowboys. He was usually an old cowhand.

▲ This map of the main cowboy trails out of Texas cannot show the thousand minor trails. The most famous trail of all was the Chisholm Trail to Abilene, first of the great Kansas cowtowns. One historian has claimed that the Chisholm carried 'the greatest migration of domestic animals known in world history'.

▶ Some cowboys called a stampede a 'stompede' but the result was the same. It usually happened at night when riding fast was highly hazardous, and blinding rain could make the trail hand's job even more difficult as he strove to get the wild longhorns into a circle. Even the snort of a horse or the smell of a strange animal could start a stampede.

TRAILS
Western
Chisholm
Shawnee
Goodnight-Loving
Railroad

GULF OF MEXICO

Chicago
Cheyenne
Ogallala
Omaha
Denver
Abilene
St Louis
Dodge
Dallas
Houston

Trail drives were the high spot of a cowboy's life. Indians and outlaws were only two of the hazards. Prairie storms, including hailstorms complete with huge stones, were a constant threat, along with lightning, while river crossings could be disastrous. However treacherous the crossing, the trail boss had to keep the longhorns on the move all the time to prevent a dreaded water stampede.

A stampede on land was the really great hazard, however. Somehow, when the shout of 'Stampede!' rang out, the cowboys had to force the longhorns into a huge circle which would finally slow them down, perhaps days later. Then rustlers might start the whole nightmare again. Many a fine cowboy died in a stampede and was buried on the prairie.

Some 10 million cattle went north up the trails between 1867 and 1890, by which time the longhorns had given way to new breeds. And by the 1890s, as we shall see, barbed wire had transformed the cowboy's West. Within a decade some of them were herding – and even eating – sheep!

A chuck wagon

▶ At the head of a herd on the march rode two experienced cowboys called pointers. Behind them at intervals came the swing men on each side. Further back were the flank men and at the rear came the drag men to pick up any stragglers. Because they had to 'eat dust' they took the job in turn. Meanwhile the trail boss was out in front, looking for watering places.

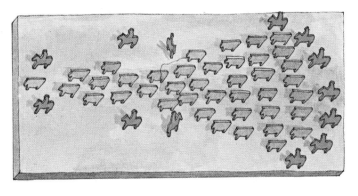

▲ Charles Russell's painting, 'Smoke of a .45'. When cowboys reached town after long months on the trail, they wanted to enjoy themselves. But enjoyment, drinking and cards could lead to sudden volcanic quarrels, gunsmoke, and a scene like this. Note the details in Russell's picture: the bottle on the ground, the scattered cards, the wooden gambling hall named The Palace!

The lawmen

Shoot-out at high noon, the Code of the West, the fast draw: these are part of the legendary West that everyone knows. But what was the Wild West of the gunfighters really like, and why was it so wild?

The United States came into being violently and, as the pioneers pushed westwards, violence was for some a way of life. It was certainly so for the Mountain Men. In many of the mining areas, too, the Law was in short supply unless ordinary citizens banded together as vigilantes. The trouble was that 'lynch law' often saw the wrong people hanged.

Before and during the Civil War (1861–65) Kansas and other western states were terrorized by marauding guerilla bands pillaging under the guise of patriotism; and it was after the war in Kansas that the Western lawman came into his own in the wild cowtowns. The first successful marshal of Abilene was Tom Smith, who in 1870 kept order not with a six-gun but with his sledgehammer fists. This remarkable town-tamer, murdered out of season by a settler, was succeeded by a very different type of marshal, Wild Bill Hickok, who was also successful in a more traditional gun-toting manner.

▶ Films have given the impression that all Western lawmen wore a 'tin star'. This was not so. However, the US Marshal's badge shown here is certainly a star, and of far more simple design than many Western badges. The US Marshal was the most important lawman in a state or territory, and senior to county sheriffs and town marshals and their deputies. The badge on the far right is that of a county sheriff – of Esmeralda County, Nevada. His deputy probably had a similar badge.

The simple but much feared badge of a US Marshal.

▲ A group of cowhands stage a mock hanging. Lynching was quite common in the West, when people were not always willing to wait for official lawmen and a judge. Many innocent men perished in this way.

▼ Fast draw: fanning. *1* Note left hand. *2* Index finger in guard holding back trigger; left palm forcing hammer back. *3* Left hand cocks hammer. *4* Pistol is cocked and fired; hammer is slapped (fanned) with left palm until all shots are fired.

A more elaborate badge for the sheriff of a small town.

▼ Below is a group that never was! Our artist has gathered together some notable lawmen connected with the Kansas cowtowns. From left to right: Wyatt Earp, once an Assistant Marshal of Dodge City; Tom Smith, who in 1870 tamed Abilene with his sledgehammer fists; Edward Masterson, Marshal of Dodge in 1878 when he was murdered; and Charles Bassett, another Dodge City lawman. Not a bunch of men to tangle with, even if history has been bent a little to line them up together.

Although Hollywood has shown us innumerable gunfighter duels, most gunfights were lethal affairs at short range or sordid scuffles in dark alleys. But Hickok did once fight a duel in the cinematic tradition, facing one Dave Tutt on the town square of Springfield, Missouri. Tutt shot first, missed and was hit in the heart by Hickok, who then rounded on his victim's friends enquiring: 'Aren't you satisfied, gentlemen? Put up your shootin' irons, or there'll be more dead men here.'

Lawmen in towns nearly always had deputies to support them; the Lone Sheriff or Marshal is a myth. But individuals did pull off astounding feats, as when Sheriff Perry Owens took on a whole houseful of killers from the outside, killed three of them, wounded a fourth and walked away without a scratch.

As for the fast draw, so beloved of Hollywood, again, it was largely a myth. True, top 'shootists' drew fast, but speed was less important than accuracy. Today's 'fast draws', unlike the bygone lawmen, do not have to face up to a John Wesley Hardin or a Billy the Kid, out to kill them. Whatever else can be said about them, the lawmen of the Wild West did not lack courage.

▲ Judge Roy Bean dispensed justice of a sort from this Texas saloon, although he was totally unqualified to do so. He named the saloon 'The Jersey Lily' after the English actress from Jersey, Lillie Langtry, whom he adored from afar.

▼ Another popular fast draw method: 1 Note butt, half way between wrist and elbow. 2 Gun is grasped with thumb over hammer and index finger outside guard. 3 Index finger slips into guard; thumb cocks hammer. 4 Gun is fired coming up.

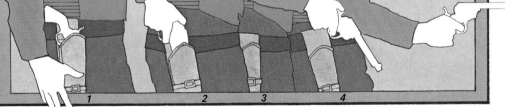

1   2   3   4

The badmen – and women

There were the robber gangs and there were the individual killers. The most notorious of the gangs were those led by Jesse and Frank James and their relatives, the Youngers. Because they had served on the Southern side in the Civil War, many people in Missouri, a Southern state, regarded them as heroes not villains, and secretly supported them. Not until a disastrous raid on a bank at Northfield, Minnesota, in 1876 did the combined James and Younger gangs come to grief. Jesse was later killed by an ex-member of his gang, Bob Ford, who shot him from behind as he stood on a chair to adjust a picture.

Jesse was no Robin Hood as some claimed, but even the majority who now paint his character very black agree that he and his men were made worse by the times they lived in. This applies to nearly all the badmen of the Wild West. It certainly applied to John Wesley Hardin, the Texan preacher's son who boasted of killing 44 men; for Texas, which fought for the South, was harshly ruled by the North in the years that followed the Civil War, and there was injustice in plenty. Yet quick-tempered Hardin would probably have been a menace in any age. He was finally shot from behind after a long spell in prison.

$25,000 REWARD
JESSE JAMES
DEAD OR ALIVE

$15,000 REWARD FOR FRANK JAMES

$5000 Reward for any Known Member of the James Band

SIGNED:

ST. LOUIS MIDLAND RAILROAD

Jesse James
Born in 1843, Jesse James graduated from guerilla fighting in the Civil War to leading a notorious band of bank and train robbers.

John Wesley Hardin
Born in Texas in 1853, John Wesley Hardin was one of the West's most deadly killers. He eventually became a lawyer.

Belle Starr
Belle Starr was a flashy female who liked cattle rustling and the company of outlaws. She met a violent end in 1889.

One of the West's choicest villains, Henry Plummer, operated in the goldfields of Montana and Idaho during the Civil War. He ran a gang of highwaymen, even having spies in hostels along the road who marked any stagecoaches worth robbing. As a precaution, he managed to become sheriff of the town from which he ruled his criminal empire, and he lasted many months before being found out and 'strung up' by vigilantes. Another crooked lawman was Marshal Henry Newton Brown, who left his job as a sheriff in Caldwell, Kansas, to raid a bank at Medicine Lodge. There were no survivors.

Between raids, or when pursued, outlaws took refuge in secret hideouts, whose whereabouts were known only to members of their gang. Here they recovered, waited for any wounds to heal, and plotted their next move. The best hideouts for badmen were in Indian Territory, later Oklahoma, into which intrepid US Marshals, alone or at the head of posses, went after the outlaws who infested the territory. Filmgoers will recall John Wayne in *True Grit* and the authentic scenes back in Fort Smith, Arkansas, where captives were hanged, often in groups, after a trial under 'Hanging Judge' Parker.

This infamous judge was, in fact, a good friend of the Indians whose territory was being misused by the badmen. His ruthlessness could be justified in the context of the West: he was fighting a war against outlawry which he had to win.

There are many myths about gunfighters. After the introduction of metallic cartridges, for example, few bothered to wear two guns. A gunfighter needed a reserve in the early days of 'cap and ball' pistols that took a long time to load and were likely to jam. But the second was a reserve to use against a mass of men or in a saloon brawl. Only a dozen or so gunfighters could shoot with both hands. And most gunfighters walked into action with the guns already poised in their hands before even they reached the danger zone. They would not risk waiting until they met their opponent before drawing their gun – despite what the movies show!

Butch Cassidy
Butch Cassidy was not a killer. But most of his Wild Bunch were far less likeable. He excelled in the art of train robbery.

REWARD
$10,000
IN GOLD COIN
Will be paid by the U. S. Government for the apprehension
DEAD OR ALIVE
of
SAM and BELLE STARR
Wanted for Robbery, Murder, Treason and other acts against the peace and dignity of the U. S.
THOMAS CRAIL
Major, 8th Missouri Cavalry, Commanding

Famous guns of the West

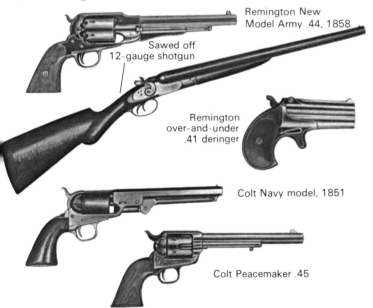

Remington New Model Army .44, 1858

Sawed off 12-gauge shotgun

Remington over-and-under .41 deringer

Colt Navy model, 1851

Colt Peacemaker .45

◀ On the opposite page one of Charles Russell's most famous paintings shows cowboys shooting it out with gamblers. Its title is 'When Guns Speak, Death Settles Disputes'.

▶ Calamity Jane enjoying a drink with some friends in 1897. One writer said of her: 'She swore, she drank, she wore men's clothing . . . She was just 50 years ahead of her time.'

Billy the Kid

Robin Hood or frontier fiend? The arguments still rage about Billy the Kid, who is – wrongly – said to have killed 21 men for every one of his 21 years, and wrongly said to have been left-handed: an early photograph of him was printed in reverse!

Billy's origins are obscure. He was born in 1859 either in New York or Indiana, and went West with his mother and brother as a boy. He did not, as is alleged, kill a 'filthy loafer' who insulted his mother when he was 12. In fact, his first killing was in Silver City, New Mexico, in 1877, when he was set on by a bully named Frank 'Windy' Cahill and shot him. Although a witness vouched it was self-defence, Billy was arrested. He escaped and signed up with a British rancher named John Tunstall in Lincoln County.

But Tunstall was a doomed man. Unscrupulous rivals arranged to have him murdered, and this triggered off the Lincoln County War, described on pages 38–39. Billy is said to have sworn an oath of vengeance over the dead body of his employer, and by the end of the war had made his name as a gunfighter.

He was on the losing side, however. With the county given over to murder, pillage and anarchy, he formed his own band of outlaws. One of the reasons for his success was that the ordinary people of Lincoln County liked him and helped him. He was finally arrested by an old friend turned sheriff, Pat Garrett. Because he had killed a lawman in the war, he was sentenced to hang and confined in the Lincoln County courthouse.

▲ While in jail in Santa Fé Billy the Kid bombarded Governor Lew Wallace with letters. He signed the letters 'Bonney', his family name.

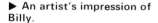

▶ An artist's impression of Billy.

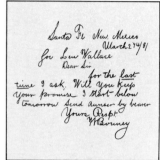

▲ A last threatening letter. When Billy the Kid's pleas went unheeded he killed two guards and made his escape.

▶ This photograph of Billy the Kid was originally printed the wrong way round; people thought he was left-handed.

These two drawings show two of the most famous incidents in the Billy the Kid saga. They appeared in his 'Life' by Pat Garrett and, unlike much of the text, are considered to be accurate.

◀ Billy kills Deputy Olinger before making his daring escape from Lincoln jail.

▶ Pat Garrett shoots Billy down in Pete Maxwell's bedroom at Fort Sumner. Garrett had been humiliated by Billy's earlier escape, and now he had his revenge. Yet many of the ordinary people of Lincoln County mourned the dead youth.

Guarded night and day by deputies Bell and Olinger, and manacled hand and foot, Billy needed outside help in order to escape. One of his friends managed to hide a pistol in the privy in the yard and got a secret note to him with the word 'privy' written on it. While Olinger was over the road guarding the other prisoners as they ate, Billy asked Bell if he could go to the privy. Coming back, he slipped his handcuffs over his narrow wrists, hit Bell with his chains, then shot him. He seized a shotgun from Garrett's office, stood at a window, and when Olinger appeared from the restaurant, shouted 'Hullo, Bob', before blasting him with buckshot. He then told the janitor to get him a file and a horse, shook hands with the onlookers, and rode out of town. His name rang round the nation.

But Billy's luck was running out. Pat Garrett, smarting under his humiliation, set out after him and finally tracked him down to Fort Sumner. In July 1881 he shot him dead in the house of a friend. The local people gave Billy a fine funeral, and though Pat Garrett became a celebrity, not everyone thought him a hero. He, too, was to die of a gunshot wound in 1908.

And how many people had Billy, the scourge of the Southwest, actually killed? It is certainly true that he was a dangerous young man and a crack shot. However, although he had taken part in five killings in the Lincoln County War, his only known solo killing remains that first one of all! Billy the Kid's renown as a daring outlaw was due mostly to the times and the place in which he lived.

◀ An artist's impression of Pat Garrett.

▼ The cover of 'A life of Billy the Kid' by Pat Garrett. Unfortunately the story he wrote is more fiction than fact.

Range wars

Large-scale feuds were frequent in the Wild West. One of the most famous was the Lincoln County War, mentioned previously in the story of Billy the Kid. Two ruthless businessmen, Murphy and Dolan, with powerful political friends, and with rustlers and outlaws in their pay, had most of Lincoln County 'sewn up'. They ran their 'kingdom' from a store called the House. Small ranchers and settlers were forced to sell property and cattle to them at low prices, while local Indians were robbed of their rations.

An enterprising young Briton, John Tunstall, and a Canadian lawyer, Alexander McSween, challenged them and started their own store near the House. The result was explosive! Tunstall was gunned down by a posse of Murphy men, and Tunstall's cowboys set out to avenge him. The climax came in a five-day street battle. Finally, the Murphy men managed to set fire to McSween's store, where Billy the Kid had taken command. Mrs McSween escaped, but her husband, unarmed, was shot down. Billy survived the fusillade. All the while, a detachment of soldiers from a local fort observed the action, officially neutral but secretly siding with the Murphy gang. Sad to say, in this case crime paid, and Dolan became an even greater power in New Mexico.

Wyoming's Johnson County War of 1892 was a classic confrontation between cattlemen, and small ranchers and farmers. The cattle barons falsely claimed that their enemies were all rustlers; in fact they wanted an excuse to seize the settlers' land. Having failed to frighten them by small-scale atrocities, they hired a force of 52 gunfighters to 'invade' Johnson County and wipe them out. Newspaper men accompanied the force under the impression that the 'enemy' were indeed guilty, while the cattle barons convinced politicians in Wyoming and Washington of the same thing. But they chose a bad first target, a lion of a man called Nate Champion. They surrounded his hut, killed his friend Nick Rae, but took a whole day to finish off Nate, only subduing him by setting fire to his hut. He dashed out to his death.

Meanwhile two passers-by had alerted the people of Johnson County, and the invaders in turn found themselves besieged and had to be rescued by the army. The cattlemen's influence was so strong that the invaders escaped, but the ordinary people of Johnson County knew they had won the day. They read Nate Champion's diary, and sang a song about him based on the words he had written. He had indeed been their champion.

▶ When it was first introduced barbed wire was a constant source of conflict in the West. Cattlemen didn't like it because it hemmed in their herds. And settlers often had disputes about their boundaries. Here one group have decided to take the law into their own hands — having first suitably disguised themselves.

▼ How cattle brands were changed. Cattle were identified by their brands, but it was not very difficult to change them, as rustlers well knew.

▲ Nate Champion (mounted nearest the chuck wagon) was the supreme hero of the Johnson County War. He met a hero's death defending his cabin against a 50-strong posse of killers hired by Wyoming's cattle kings.

▶ Rough justice in the Wild West. A posse ride out to catch a lawbreaker — who may or may not get a fair trial when they find him.

The Pony Express

It was the most thrilling relay race in history. A notice appeared in a San Francisco paper in 1860 calling for 'young skinny, wiry fellows, not over 18'; the short but glorious saga of the Pony Express had begun.

In the 1850s, booming gold-rich California urgently needed a fast mail service to link up with the rest of the USA 3,200 kilometres to the east. The Butterfield Overland Mail took about 25 days to reach California after swinging far south, so the firm of Russell, Majors and Waddell decided to set up a direct, central mail route. Amazingly, they did so in only 60 days. They built 190 stations across the West at regular intervals, bought 500 wiry Indian ponies, and took on 80 riders. Seventy-five horses were to be used in each direction for a run. At every station, the rider would be allowed just two minutes to swing his saddlebag on to a new mount and gallop away again. After a fixed distance one rider would hand the mail over to the next until they reached Sacramento, California. From there the mail would be rushed by steamboat through to San Francisco.

The young riders were forbidden to swear or drink, and each of them was given a Bible to carry. Letters had to be written on thin paper protected from bad weather by oilcloth, and telegrams were also carried in special saddlebags.

The great adventure began at St Joseph, Missouri, on 3 April 1860. That first run took just 10 days. When the mail reached San Francisco, the excited inhabitants laid on a grand parade: their years of isolation were ending. Pony Express riders had to average 14 kilometres an hour, though some managed over 30. In places the terrain was very rugged, so daily distances could vary between 60 and 120 kilometres. On one epic occasion a team got through in a mere six days.

The firm's ponies were so swift that the boy riders could usually outrace hostile Indians, who tended to concentrate their attacks on the stations along the route. It was in and around these that the Pony Express suffered its worst casualties.

The Pony Express riders had special lightweight saddles, only a third as heavy as normal Western saddles. The leather *mochila* with four mail pouches had cutouts to fit around the pommel and cantle. When the rider was changing mounts it could be swung very quickly from one horse to another – in far less time in fact than the regulation two minutes allowed for a rider at a Pony Express station along his route. The telegrams and letters carried were enclosed in oilcloth as a protection against the weather.

A Pony Express saddle

Most of the young riders survived their heroic journey, and those that failed died hard. At a Nevada station the hands saw a pony dash up, its rider slumped over the saddle horn. His body was riddled with arrows, but he was clutching his horse's mane so grimly that it had to be hacked from his dead grasp.

The Pony Express lasted only 18 months. It collapsed overnight with the completion of the transcontinental telegraph which made it superfluous. Russell, Waddell and Majors lost a fortune, for their fabulous service cost far more to run than could be charged. Yet the Pony Express – which carried 34,753 items of mail – achieved world-wide fame and remains one of the West's most thrilling adventures.

▲ A Pony Express rider being chased by Indians. Although this was an ever-present hazard for the young riders, they were usually able to escape from the Indians – thanks to the superior speed of their well-fed horses. One young veteran recalled: 'Grain-fed muscles got me out of the danger of their arrows and the few old guns they had. Their grass-fed ponies couldn't keep me long in gun-shot'.

▲ A Pony Express recruiting poster. Pony Express riders had to be young, fit, and not too large!

◀ A striking painting by Frederic Remington of a scene at a Pony Express station. One rider has just reached the station and another is already galloping off with the mail.

41

Riverboats

For some 60 years steamboats ruled the waters of the Mississippi, Missouri and other Western rivers. Some were floating palaces, others were more like armoured gunboats prepared for instant action against the Indians. Even the least elaborate of them looked impressive, with smoke erupting from their tall funnels and their paddles flashing in the sun.

Life on board a steamboat in the heyday of river traffic was varied and exciting. Gamblers and dancing girls, businessmen and crooks, families and sightseers all travelled by steamboat. And the steamboats carried cargo too: cotton, coal, and every conceivable sort of trading good.

The Steamboat Age began when the *New Orleans* started trading between New Orleans and Natchez, Mississippi, in 1811, and by 1840 its peak had been reached. The decline began in the 1870s when railroads overtook them as both freight and passenger carriers. Today, though big modern barges carry goods on the rivers, the only steamboats that survive are glamorous tourist vessels.

The captain-owners of the steamboats were kings of the river. They thought nothing of spending a fortune on furnishings, for they could recover their costs in a single season, and they often hired first-class entertainment for their passengers too.

As well as fine navigators, they also had to be bankers and merchants. Plantation owners would hand over their entire stocks of cotton or sugar to be sold by the captain at the best price down river. Ranchers and farmers trusted them too. In 1846, 1,190 steamboats carried 400 million dollars' worth of goods on the Western rivers; some years later the lower Missouri was even busier than the Mississippi. Rivalling the captains in importance were the pilots who had to steer the vessels. They needed a cool head: the humorous writer Mark Twain called the Mississippi the crookedest river in the world.

Many steamboats burnt wood, many more burnt coal, and all were liable to blow up. 'They generally blow up forwards', a passenger told the novelist Charles Dickens in 1842.

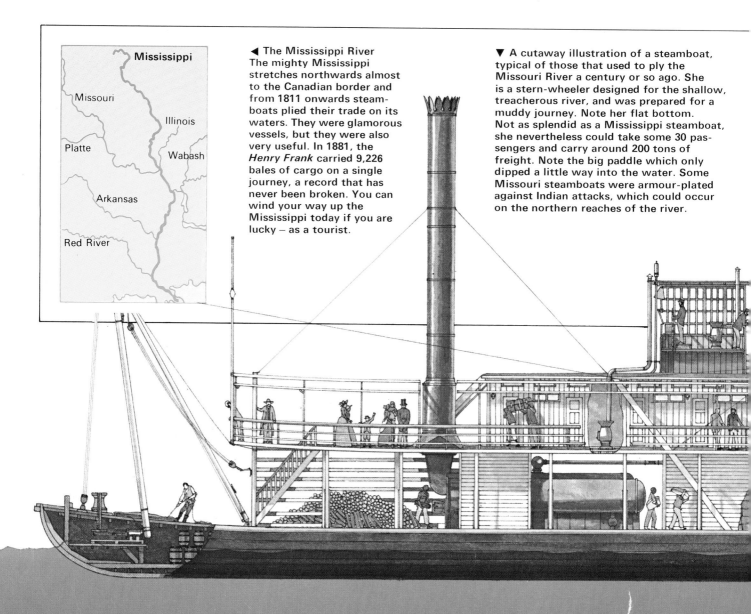

◀ **The Mississippi River** The mighty Mississippi stretches northwards almost to the Canadian border and from 1811 onwards steamboats plied their trade on its waters. They were glamorous vessels, but they were also very useful. In 1881, the *Henry Frank* carried 9,226 bales of cargo on a single journey, a record that has never been broken. You can wind your way up the Mississippi today if you are lucky – as a tourist.

Map labels: Mississippi, Missouri, Illinois, Platte, Wabash, Arkansas, Red River

▼ A cutaway illustration of a steamboat, typical of those that used to ply the Missouri River a century or so ago. She is a stern-wheeler designed for the shallow, treacherous river, and was prepared for a muddy journey. Note her flat bottom. Not as splendid as a Mississippi steamboat, she nevertheless could take some 30 passengers and carry around 200 tons of freight. Note the big paddle which only dipped a little way into the water. Some Missouri steamboats were armour-plated against Indian attacks, which could occur on the northern reaches of the river.

Steamboat races were always popular, though they greatly increased the chances of blowing up. The most famous race took place in 1870, when the *Natchez* raced the *Robert E. Lee* from New Orleans to St Louis on the Mississippi. To the delight of millions of Southerners who worshipped their Civil War leader it was the *Lee* that won.

But a far greater race happened in 1876, after General Custer and his command had been annihilated (see page 54). Captain Grant Marsh of the *Far West* learnt that survivors of Custer's regiment needed to be rushed 1,136 kilometres down the Big Horn River, the Yellowstone and the Missouri to medical help at Fort Lincoln. Through rough and raging waters, the *Far West* averaged 560 kilometres a day. Fifty-one of the wounded survived and Grant Marsh's speed record was never broken.

The last fling of the Steamboat Age took place during the Klondike stampede of 1898. For a year or two steamboats sailed up the mighty Yukon River. But the days of their glory were really over.

▲ The *Bessie*, on the Rio Grande in Texas, stopping for a short halt at Fort Rignold in 1890. Most steamboats were essentially working craft. The glamour and luxury they provided for some of their passengers was not as important to their survival as the essential role they played in linking towns and counties and states, carrying goods for sale. By the 1870s, however, they were beginning to lose trade to the new railroads.

▶ The Missouri River
The Missouri was the great river of the West. Lewis and Clark had headed up it in their epic journey to the Pacific, and it played a key role in the taming of the West. The only good thing about this tricky river, from a shipowner's point of view, was that it was so shallow that many wrecks were later salvaged. It took all a pilot's skill to steer a boat from one end to the other without mishap.

Stagecoach kings

Long after the stagecoach had vanished from the rest of the USA, it was still found all over the West. Not until the 1890s did it finally disappear, having lasted in the West almost until the age of the motor car.

Stagecoach travel was not as Western films suggest. There were plenty of hold-ups, but it took a daring band to challenge the 'Queen of the Prairies', a Concord coach, which might have up to 18 people aboard, many of them heavily armed.

The drivers were often even more colourful than their Hollywood equivalents. One of them, 'One-eyed' Charlie Parkhurst, a pistol-packing hard case known as the 'greatest whip in the West', was unique. When Charlie died, it transpired that 'he' was a woman!

Travel, if only occasionally dangerous, was highly uncomfortable. The roads varied from barely adequate to non-existent, and the journeys were slow. One helpful newspaper cautioned prospective travellers: 'Don't discuss politics or religion.' Tempers could flare easily in the cramped confinement of a coach.

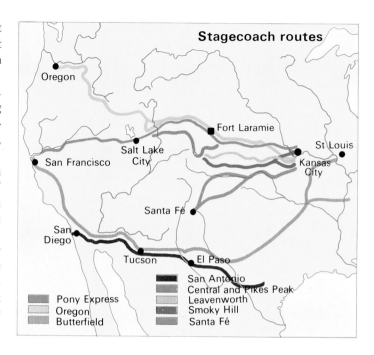

Stagecoach routes

Oregon
Fort Laramie
St Louis
Salt Lake City
San Francisco
Kansas City
Santa Fé
San Diego
Tucson
El Paso
San Antonio

Pony Express
Oregon
Butterfield
Central and Pikes Peak
Leavenworth
Smoky Hill
Santa Fé

A Wells Fargo coach

The first transcontinental stage line was organized by John Butterfield in 1858. Twice a week his stagecoaches set out on an immense journey of some 4,500 kilometres from St Louis, Missouri, down into the Southwest, where they braved the perils of Apache territory, then up to Los Angeles and San Francisco in California. Butterfield built resting stations every 32 kilometres and ran 250 coaches. The mammoth journey took about 25 days, provided circumstances were favourable.

Ben Holladay, a rugged and independent character, became the next 'Stagecoach King'. He bought up Butterfield's empire and expanded it to serve the new booming mining towns and small frontier communities in the West.

Holladay believed in leading from the front. Sometimes he drove his own coaches himself or, more often, he rode shotgun. On one occasion, single-handed, he drove off a band of Sioux. Soon he was popularly known as the Napoleon of the West.

In 1866, Ben Holladay sold his stagecoach empire at a vast profit and put his money into railroads instead. His buyers were two friends from the East who had come up the hard way in the stagecoach business, as messengers and drivers. Their names were Henry Wells and William Fargo, and together they built up the greatest stagecoach network known in the United States, probably in the world.

Shrewdly, when the railroads threatened to ruin their livelihood, they moved into that field as well, then into banking. Today the firm they founded continues in the travel business, and is part of the American Express Company – which in turn was founded by the original Butterfield.

Stagecoaches today are as dead as clipper ships. They have no role to play in a modern transport system. Thanks to films however, they are not forgotten, even if advice like, 'Don't point out where murders have been committed, especially if there are women passengers', no longer applies in quite the same way!

◀ This coach, one of the Wells Fargo fleet of stagecoaches, was a Concord, one of the most famous vehicles in American history. Four or six horses pulled it, and no less than 21 passengers could be carried, 9 inside on the padded benches and 12 out on the roof. With the driver sat an express messenger riding 'shotgun', and the pair sat on a seat under which was a 'boot' which contained valuables and mail. There was a bigger boot at the back.

The stagecoach was strongly built, but comfortable: the carriage was suspended on two 'thoroughbraces'. These were shock-absorbers made of thick strips of leather. The coach rocked too much for some travellers, but the humorous writer, Mark Twain, was not being funny when he called the Concord 'a cradle on wheels'. The coach was named after the town of Concord where it was built.

'It don't break down: it only wears out', said stagecoach men, though some of them would not even accept that it wore out. One coach sank, was recovered after a month, and remained in service for 50 years!

With so many passengers on board, there were plenty of guns in case of attack.

250 craftsmen produced some 2,000 Concords every year.

▶ There were plenty of robbers eager to hold up stagecoaches, especially ones carrying gold or silver. Wells Fargo suffered greatly until their detectives under the remarkable James Hume managed to break the power of the gangs. The biggest loss ever suffered by the firm was 80,000 dollars, stolen from a coach by one Rattlesnake Dick!

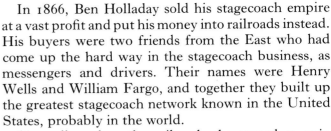

REWARD

WELLS, FARGO & CO.'S EXPRESS BOX on COAST LINE STAGE CO'S ROUTE, from Soledad, was ROBBED this morning, by two men, about ten miles north of San Miguel.

$250 Each

will be paid for ARREST and CONVICTION of the Robbers.

San Francisco, July 15, 1875.   JNO. J. VALENTINE, Gen. Supt.

▼ A painting by Charles Russell captures the dangerous flavour of a hold-up. The sign says '20 miles to Deadwood', which suggests the hold-up occurred in the Black Hills of South Dakota, excellent ambush country! Deadwood was a rough mining town but plenty of gold was carried from it and provided a good lure for 'road agents'.

45

The coming of the railroad

In 1862, while the Civil War was raging, an act was passed by the American Congress authorizing the building of a railroad from the Missouri River to Sacramento in California. However, not until the guns fell silent in 1865 could proper work on the great adventure begin.

Two companies were involved. The Union Pacific headed westwards from Omaha, Nebraska, while over 3,000 kilometres away, the Central Pacific was heading eastwards. Thousands of construction workers were needed by both companies. The Central Pacific's construction boss, Charley Crocker, found that most white men were too busy trying to find gold to want to work at an even more rugged job, so he hired a number of Chinese coolies, who quickly proved their worth in the harsh and difficult work.

The Union Pacific's work force was more mixed, but fortunately included plenty of Civil War veterans – for the Sioux and Cheyennes fiercely resented the iron road that was being laid across their hunting grounds. Isolated advance parties were under constant threat of attack, bridge-builders were a special target, and the Indians also ripped up rails and sometimes derailed trains.

The two lines finally met on 10 May 1869 at Promontory Point in Utah. The solemn moment was marked by the driving in of a ceremonial 'golden spike', and the entire nation rejoiced – rightly, for this greatest engineering feat in American history had for the first time securely linked the West to the rest of the USA. The direct result was the opening up of the plains and prairies by settlers who came first in their thousands and then in millions. The only losers were the Indians, for troop trains could now carry their enemies swiftly to them, and the great herds of buffalo who had once roamed the Plains were rapidly decimated by the white hunters riding on the 'iron horse'.

The building of the transcontinental railroad and other railroads in the West made the businessmen who put up the money even richer than they had been. Yet these 'Robber Barons', so named because of their often dubious business methods, helped to mould America. The true railroad heroes, however, were the workers. They pitted their lives against mountains, torrents, avalanches, snows, floods and deserts. They fought off Indian attacks, and they endured unending, often back-breaking, work. While their names are forgotten, their achievement is not.

◄ A vivid impression of a train being ambushed by Indians. Indians soon realized that the iron rails threatened their way of life, and waged constant warfare against the railways. The Union Pacific suffered so much from Indian attacks while it was being built that thousands of troops were sent to defend both workers and trains.

▲ This painting by Thomas Otter, 'On the Road', brings together the two forms of transport that did most to open up the West: the prairie wagon and the train. Wagons continued to be used in parts of the West well into this century.

▼ A poster inviting settlers to travel west by rail.

The end of an era

When did the Old West of the white man really end? Some say it was in 1892, when the government announced that there was no more first-rate free land to be given away to settlers – just over 30 years after its declaration that anyone could claim 160 acres for a filing fee of 10 dollars. The only requirement was that the claimant lived on the land and farmed it for five years. Now there was no more good land left.

The gunfighters' West finally ended around the turn of the century. As good a date as any is 1902, when Butch Cassidy and the Sundance Kid of Wild Bunch fame left the USA for South America. Holding up trains had ceased to be as profitable as once it had been, though one of the Bunch, Ben Kilpatrick, the Tall Texan, tried his hand at the old sport as late as 1912 and perished for his pains.

Now real towns dotted the Great Plains, most notably Denver on the edge of the Rockies. Meanwhile what were once the Kansas cowtowns had been sober for many years – literally. Frightened by bad publicity about the sinfulness and godlessness of the cowtowns, the state authorities had in the 1880s declared Kansas 'dry', which meant that no liquor could be sold there. The edict shook old-timers but certainly helped to attract settlers.

Barbed wire was introduced in the mid-1870s. Enclosing the Great Plains helped to settle them, even though cattlemen rebelled against the ending of the old free-for-all open range. Much blood flowed and much wire was cut, but the cattle barons eventually saw the advantage of fencing. Legal rights to land were drawn up and selective breeding of cattle became easier and more profitable.

New breeds of cattle were introduced. Herefords were shipped to Texas as early as the 1870s and by the 1890s the famous XIT ranch had no less than 3,000 Hereford and Angus bulls. The pure longhorn gradually disappeared from the West. It was replaced either by crossbred cows which retained some of the longhorn strain, or by imported quality breeds. Herefords were the most successful British imports. Today the only surviving longhorns – occasionally seen in films – are kept as living museums of a glorious past, or as pets by rich ranch owners.

And the unfortunate sheepmen? The last massacre of men and beasts by irate cowboys appears to have been in Wyoming in 1909, but by that time most cattlemen had ceased to hate the 'woollies', and some cowboys were actually to be seen herding the once loathed sheep. Times were changing indeed.

Meanwhile bicycles had appeared in the West, to be followed at the turn of the century by the first noisy motor cars. The old order stuck out for as long as it could, but the West had really been tamed once communication with the East had been made swift and efficient.

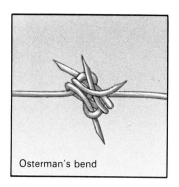

▶ Different types of barbed wire. The first barbed wire was introduced in the West in the mid-1870s, and had immediate and far-reaching effects.

Barbed wire was made in all sorts of ways, and there were more than 1,000 types. Some of them, as you can see, were rather fantastic. Barbed wire collecting has become a great hobby in the USA.

Osterman's bend

▲ 'The Fall of the Cowboy', a painting by Remington. By the 1890s the great age of the cowboy was coming to an end.

▼ 'Country School', by E. L. Henry. Children recite their lessons. Much school work in the God-fearing West was based on a study of the Bible.

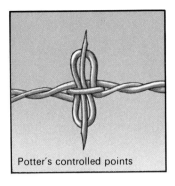

Potter's controlled points

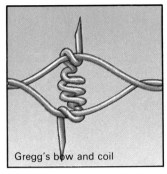

Gregg's bow and coil

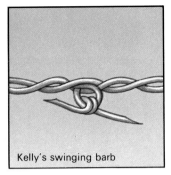

Kelly's swinging barb

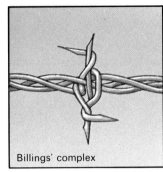

Billings' complex

▶ This advertisement for settlers was enough to make an old-timer spill his drink, for it noted as an attraction that there were no saloons. Northern Kansas had gone 'dry'. It had had its share of drunken cowboys and other Frontier gentry (and incidentally, had made a lot of money out of them). Now it was sobering up.

▼ Schoolchildren photographed outside their newly-built schoolhouse in Alma, Wisconsin, 1897. Instead of a one-room shack managed by a single teacher (see left), this schoolhouse is a solid well-built structure, designed for a large number of children. As more and more families (rather than single men) settled in the West, towns became more respectable, and churches and schools were built instead of saloons.

"Ad astra per aspera"

Northern Kansas.

AN INVITATION

IS HEREBY EXTENDED TO EVERYBODY DESIRING A CHOICE HOME IN THE

FINEST COUNTRY IN THE WORLD,

◆ COME ◆

To Northern Kansas

And Locate in the State that is

ALWAYS AT THE FRONT.

BRING YOUR FAMILY

To the State that offers you FERTILE LANDS, PROSPEROUS TOWNS, plenty of CHURCHES and SCHOOLS, and

NO SALOONS.

▲ This photograph of a car going through a hole carved in a redwood tree in the Yosemite National Park, California, was taken about 70 years ago — surely proof that the Wild West had been tamed!

Today the national parks are one of the few places where visitors can glimpse what the West was like before the white men arrived.

49

The losers

Not everyone gained from the civilizing of the Wild West. But none lost quite as much as the Indians.

The Indians have been shadowy figures throughout this book. They were in the West before the white man, and they continued to live there after he came – though their life was never the same again. The white men who visited the Plains in the 1840s were fascinated by the Indians' way of life; and the Indians, not yet feeling threatened, welcomed them. But the warning signs were there. Tribes from the South were already being driven into Indian Territory, now Oklahoma, either because their land was needed by settlers or because gold had been found. Meanwhile, the Plains Indians watched as the wagon trains went through; while in California, after gold had been found, total disaster overtook tribe after tribe and many were exterminated.

Out on the Plains, the Indians were at the heyday of their glory. Rejoicing in their horses, they fought like medieval knights, counting it greater honour to touch an enemy than to kill him. They enjoyed horse-stealing even more than fighting. But the days of their freedom were numbered. By the 1870s, the seemingly limitless buffalo herds were beginning to disappear. The railroads that began to criss-cross the West brought in more hunters and more soldiers. And settlers who had once crossed to Oregon were now taking up Indian land. Suddenly, the romantic Indian was merely a nuisance who was in the way.

▼ Buffalo crossing a train line. They and the Indians who depended on them were the greatest losers in the story of the American West.

▲ 'The Song of the Talking Wire'. The coming of the telegraph speeded up communications, and brought the Indians more problems.

Some Indians opted for peace, others fought. Many tribes were divided, and some sided with the whites: the Shoshones, for example, who were being threatened by the Sioux, a much larger tribe. The Crows, too, sided with the Americans. As a result of their alliance they got better reservations than the 'hostiles', but their way of life still crumbled away.

The Indians were mystified by the white man's attitude to land. How could men own the Earth, their Mother? By tradition certain Indian tribes dominated certain areas of land, usually for hunting reasons. But they never owned it in the white sense, and even the land on which they camped belonged to the tribe.

As the years went by, and more and more white men came to the West, it gradually dawned on some tribes that the white men's numbers were limitless. A few, feeling defeated, made peace. Meanwhile the reservations allotted to them were constantly being encroached. Many tribes were driven out to much poorer lands. Some of these were in totally different climates and the Indians died of fever. They were forced to take up farming, often in poor and infertile soils.

Against this background war was inevitable – on the Plains, and in the deserts and mountains of the Southwest. For a whole generation there would be war between the white man and the Indian in the West, as the Indian fought for survival. But the wars were in the end no more than a delaying tactic – for they could have only one ending.

◀ The faces of defeat: Bannack Indians on a reservation in 1870. Their faces express their humiliation and despair.

▼ An unscrupulous pedlar tries to sell liquor to Indians on a reservation. Many tribes banned the use of alcohol.

The army in the West

Think how lost a crowd of 15,000 would be in a modern sports stadium holding up to 100,000. Yet after the Civil War ended in 1865, and hundreds of thousands of soldiers were sent home, just 15,000 regular troops were expected to police the entire region west of the Mississippi.

Their job was virtually impossible. They were ordered to protect the Indians from land-grabbing whites one minute and the next, when government policy changed, to fight the Indians. Officials back in Washington could never make up their minds for more than a few years at a time about how to solve the 'Indian problem'. Though one general is quoted as saying 'The only good Indian is a dead Indian', the troops were not the monsters that some modern films and books make them out to have been; nor were they the dashing heroes of earlier films. They were simply men doing a hard job in difficult circumstances.

Some soldiers sympathized with their enemies, some even admired them. One wrote: 'If I were an Indian, I think that I would greatly prefer to cast my lot among those of my people who adhered to the free open plains, rather than submit to the quiet, unexciting, uneventful life of a reservation.' The writer's name was Custer, perhaps the most famous Indian-fighter of them all (see page 54).

cavalry sergeant, 1860s
winter kit, 18
infantry
private, 1860s

87940

◀ The officers' quarters at Fort Marcy, New Mexico. Generally senior officers lived well even in remote outposts. In a few places, however, even the officers' quarters were just sod huts.

As for the men, their lives were considerably harsher. Below left you can see the men's quarters at the same fort – much more bleak and basic than the officers' quarters. Their food was also less good. A common joke in the army was that the cooks killed more men than the Indians did.

▲ Some of the uniforms worn by the US army in the West. On the whole the uniforms were made out of the same basic kit of pale trousers and dark shirt, with the different ranks and duties indicated by insignia on the sleeves and caps. Notice, for example, the distinctive bugle horn badge on the cap of the man on the far left: that showed he was an infantry man.

By the 1880s there were also many black regiments in the West (see far right). They were mostly cavalrymen.

artillery lieutenant,
campaign dress, 1870s

cavalry captain,
Custer's 7th Cavalry, 1876

black corporal,
10th Cavalry,
1880s

A soldier's pay was bad and promotion for officers was desperately slow. They and their men endured boredom, occasional extreme danger, every kind of weather and, if captured by certain tribes, a horrible prolonged death. They were expected to keep going, as one of their songs put it, for 'Forty miles a day on beans and hay'.

Food varied depending on the location of a post. If hunting was good in the area, the soldier's menu was good. Otherwise there was too much emphasis on salt pork or beef, hardtack (hard biscuits), and dried vegetables. Living conditions were tough. Not until after the Civil War were ranks other than officers allowed to have their wives with them on the post. It was hardly surprising that many soldiers, officers as well as men, took to drink, and that desertion was a common problem.

The US army in the West was based on a number of forts placed at strategic points. Most forts were little more than a cluster of huts, built of wood and stone. Only a few had a second storey. Garrisons varied from a dozen up to about 200 men. They sweated in summer and froze in winter.

This then was the Frontier Army. Like so much of the West, it is now legend, but once was a force of tough men doing a tough and often thankless job.

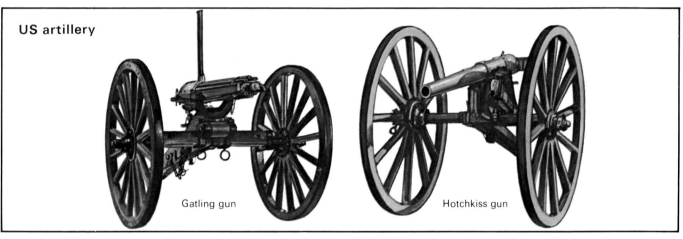

US artillery

Gatling gun

Hotchkiss gun

▲ The two most common pieces of artillery used by the army in the West. Artillery did not play a major part in the winning of the West, but it could badly frighten Indians when they first encountered it. Hotchkiss guns, for example, played havoc with the Sioux at Wounded Knee in 1890 (see page 57).

◄ The army on manoeuvre at Hidden Wood Creek. Notice how they have spread out into a fan shape for better protection against attack.

◄ Lieutenant Casey with a group of Cheyenne scouts. Although the army were fighting the Indians, they also hired a large number of Indian scouts, who proved expert at tracking down the enemy in harsh and difficult country.

Indian wars

'Good shots, good riders and the best fighters the sun ever shone on.' 'The greatest mounted fighters of all time.' These extravagant compliments were paid by officers of the US Army to the prowess of the warrior tribes of the Plains: the Sioux, Cheyennes, Blackfeet, Arapahoes and other legendary peoples against whom the white soldiers fought.

Even before the Civil War the southern Plains had been in turmoil, with Comanches and Kiowas trying to stem the white tide by using terror tactics. The Sioux in turn began to feel white pressure in the 1850s. In 1862, while the Civil War was raging in the East, the Santee Sioux in Minnesota, an already white area, became so incensed by their treatment (one agent sneered: 'If they are hungry let them eat grass!') that they rebelled, perpetrating one of the worst massacres in Western history. When it was over and their leaders had been hanged, they were driven away westwards.

Soon there was almost constant warfare, with Indians launching full-scale attacks on forts and isolated settlements, ambushing trains and travellers, and waging a fierce war of nerves; while the army retaliated with reprisal raids and a string of broken treaty agreements. Both sides believed they were in the right; both were fighting for their lives. The Indians had speed and surprise on their side. But they were gradually outnumbered and weakened by inter-tribal quarrels.

In 1866 Red Cloud's war broke out, a war the Indians won. It started dramatically with the erection in Wyoming of Fort Phil Kearny on the Bozeman Trail which led to the Montana goldfields. A hothead named Fetterman rashly boasted, 'Give me 80 men and I'll ride through the Sioux nation'. One December day he got his wish and rode out with 80 men. They were ambushed, and died to the last man. In 1868, the war ended with the evacuation of the fort and its burning down by the exultant Indians.

The most famous Indian victory of all took place at the Little Big Horn in Montana in 1876. In 1874 General Custer had led an expedition into the Black Hills, sacred to the Sioux, and there found gold. Custer, a glory-hunter not unlike a Sioux warrior in his attitude, met his end when he and 200 of his 7th Cavalry were massacred by Sioux and Cheyenne Indians under Crazy Horse, Sitting Bull and Gall. But Custer's Last Stand was also the last great stand of the Indians in the West. They could not fight in winter because of lack of supplies, the buffalo herds were vanishing, railroads spanned the West, settlers were flooding in, and suddenly the whites seemed numberless.

One by one the great fighting tribes were confined to reservations. These were sometimes formed from part, and usually the worst part, of their homeland. More often, however, the tribes were shipped off to rot in unhospitable Indian Territory.

Sitting Bull
This most famous of Sioux Indians, born in 1834, was a medicine man and warrior. He was killed on his reservation in 1890.

Red Cloud
A renowned Sioux warrior and orator, and the leading war chief of his people in the 1860s. Later, he chose the path of peace.

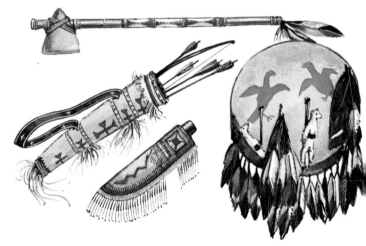

▲ Some Indian weapons: a tomahawk (top), a bow and arrows in their holder, a knife and sheath, and a beautiful shield. Such highly decorated weapons as these would probably have been used mostly on ceremonial occasions.

▼ An Indian version of Custer's Last Stand in June 1876. It was drawn by a veteran of the fight, Kicking Bear, around 1898, and is the only illustration of the battle by someone who was actually present. Custer is dressed in yellow.

Two Moon
He was the leader of the Cheyennes at the Battle of the Little Big Horn, also known as Custer's Last Stand.

Wolf Robe
Unlike the other three Indian chiefs shown here, Wolf Robe, a Cheyenne, was never famous, but he lives on in this photograph.

▲ A Sioux chief rides into battle, with his braves behind him. The Indian war-charge was a tactic to terrify the enemy.

Rearguard action

By the 1880s, nearly all the Indian tribes had been subdued – except the Apaches. These tigers of the desert terrorized whites and Indians alike. Their very name meant 'enemy' in the Zuni Indian tongue and they trained their children for war from infancy.

The Apaches did not regard war in the same way as the Sioux and Cheyennes, as a great game in which it was heroic to touch an enemy. For the Apaches war was a matter of ambush and fiendish torture. They were perhaps the greatest guerilla fighters that ever lived.

There were probably never more than 6,000 Apaches, and they were divided into a number of tribes which were rarely united. The Americans had plenty of chance of avoiding war, yet time and again the prospects of peace were thrown away by foolishness, treachery, and the greed of businessmen who made large fortunes out of supplying the troops.

The Mimbreno Apaches were the first to be driven to war: their chief was flogged for daring to watch miners at work. Then in 1861 his son-in-law Cochise of the Chiricahuas joined him. Cochise had realized that the survival of his nation depended on friendship with the whites, but a foolish young officer wrongly accused him of kidnapping a white boy and ordered his arrest. The result was the worst Indian war of the century, which lasted until 1872.

Two years after Cochise's death in 1874 his people were forced from their beloved mountains to the fever-ridden San Carlos reservation. There followed a bloody decade of break-outs and skirmishes. Dashing warriors bands created havoc wherever they rode. The only people who could track them down were Apache scouts. The final outbreak took place in March 1886. Twenty-two warriors, 13 women and 2 children, led by Geronimo, slipped from the reservation. By September it was all over. The ruthless General Miles shipped not only the hostiles to rot in a Florida prison camp but many loyal Apache scouts as well.

Meanwhile, in the Far West, the Nez Percés, who had befriended the whites since the time of Lewis and Clark, found their land needed by white settlers. Under their leader Chief Joseph, one of the noblest of all Indians, they began an epic retreat of over 3,000 kilometres eastwards, then north towards Canada and safety. Hampered by women and children, they were finally forced to surrender a few miles from freedom.

There followed the final tragedy at Wounded Knee in South Dakota. In 1890 after a series of misunderstandings, the band of the Sioux Chief Big Foot was slaughtered in the snow by the 7th Cavalry. This was a nightmarish accident rather than a planned extermination, but the result was the same: the Indian wars were finally over.

Apache braves wait in deadly ambush as the cavalry approach.

▲ The Apache leader Geronimo in suitably defiant pose.

◄ Geronimo and the last of his fighting band, photographed on their way to exile in a Florida prison camp.

▼ The dead body of the Sioux chief Big Foot lies frozen in the snow after the slaughter of his people at Wounded Knee, 1890.

The Wild West today

There are still a few 'old-timers' who remember the old days, men and women who were brought up in sod houses on the prairie, who saw gunfights, who remember the Indian wars, but their numbers are diminishing fast. The Old West is dead – or is it?

In most senses it is truly dead. Fast cars speed along highways where once pioneers struggled to cover 20 kilometres a day, and planes have virtually banished the railroads. Once wild cowtowns like Dodge City and Abilene now look like typical American towns. As for the Indians, although they are no longer a dying race, their tragedy continues. Except for a lucky few on good land or on land made rich by oil strikes, too many stagnate on arid reservations, dreaming of a past that is no longer possible. They cannot agree among themselves whether to cling to the remnants of their old life or to join the new rat race. Few are interested in money in the way whites are, but money talks.

Some Indians have made good, notably some Apaches who are now cowboys. This work suits the grandsons of matchless guerilla fighters much better than farming. Other tribes run their reservations as tourist attractions. No Indian is forced to stay on a reservation, but lack of education makes it hard for many of them to succeed away from it. Americans are now beginning to appreciate the Indian problem, and lawyers are trying to help them retain their lands. Nevertheless, the Indians, who fought valiantly for the USA in two World Wars and in Korea and Vietnam, remain second-class citizens.

So what is left of the Wild West? There are cowboys still, who are crack riders even if they sometimes drive jeeps and wear sunglasses. Many small farmers live lives not unlike those of their ancestors, for all the benefits of good housing and air conditioning, and the banishment of loneliness and distance by cars, radio and TV.

The real West, however, lingers on most clearly in the vast areas that still remain empty of people. Many of these are now national parks. See the deserts and mountains of Arizona and New Mexico and you glimpse the perils of the Apache wars; see the endless prairies and you can dimly understand what it took to cross them. In some magical places you can still stand in the wagon ruts of the Oregon Trail. And there are ghost towns, some of them in ruins, others carefully restored to capture the magic of the past.

▼ Medicine shows still tour the West, though today they are obviously a tourist 'show'. Once upon a time they used to pretend they could cure every sort of ill.

► Apache Junction in Arizona looks just like the real Old West. But it is only a movie set.

▼ A wild brahma rider is cheered by the crowds at a rodeo. The word 'rodeo' once meant simply a round-up but now it is the world famous name for an exciting Western entertainment. The chief attraction is the exercise of traditional cowboy skills against various sorts of cattle and (as here) untamed horses. Rodeos began with the end of the real Wild West. The two most famous ones are held every year in Calgary, Alberta, and Cheyenne, Wyoming.

▲ Children gaze at Navaho Indians at work in Monument Valley, Arizona. Many traditional Indian skills are now no more than a tourist attraction.

▼ Hugh Little Owl (on the right) and other members of the Crow tribe at a tribal gathering in Montana. The Crows are one of the more prosperous Indian tribes.

59

How to find out more

FILMS

The vast majority of those who become fascinated with the American West hit the trail via films. Which is not to say that many films bear much relation to the Old West: they do not. Television films, however enjoyable, are the chief culprits, for the average series is badly weakened by having to feature the same group of people every week and by shortage of time and money. The Western of the cinema is better. True, facts often take a poor second to fiction and films that claim to be the 'true story' of, say, Billy the Kid are often anything but. Some masterpieces of cinema – John Ford's *My Darling Clementine* about Wyatt Earp, for instance – are travesties of fact. Here are just a handful of Westerns to look out for, which though some of them make an epic subject too romantic, are excellent and reasonably accurate:

Mountain Men

Jeremiah Johnson (1972) starring Robert Redford, who plays a mountain man roughly based on a character called 'Liver-eating' Johnson. *Director*: Sydney Pollack.

Gold Rush

Paint Your Wagon (1969). Though a musical, this hugely entertaining film (with a classic performance by Lee Marvin) catches the atmosphere of the Californian gold rush. *Director*: Joshua Logan.

Cowboys

Red River (1948). Starring John Wayne, this is the best film about cowboys and a trail herd from Texas to Kansas. *Director*: Howard Hawks.

Will Penny (1967). Starring Charlton Heston. A gripping, down-to-earth look at the life of an ordinary, ageing cowboy. *Director*: Tom Gries.

Gunfighters

High Noon (1952). A classic starring Gary Cooper as the lone marshal facing a dangerous gang. In reality he would not have been left alone, but the film is a masterpiece. *Director*: Fred Zinnemann.

The Gunfighter (1950). Gregory Peck as an ageing gunfighter trying to avoid trouble. *Director*: Henry King.

Shane (1953). Inspired by the Johnson County War and taken from Jack Schaefer's magnificent book, this beautifully made film is many people's favourite Western. Starring Alan Ladd as Shane, it is also a tribute to the Western settlers (Van Heflin and Jean Arthur) and there is a classic badman/hired gun (Jack Palance). *Director*: George Stevens.

The Army

She Wore a Yellow Ribbon (1949). The best of all John Ford's tributes to the US Cavalry, starring John Wayne. The setting is Arizona, some of it Ford's beloved Monument Valley. *Director*: John Ford.

Indians and the Indian Wars

Broken Arrow (1950). Based on Elliott Arnold's *Blood Brother*, which itself was based on the true story of Cochise and Tom Jeffords, his white blood brother, this was the first major modern Western to put the Indian point of view. Starring James Stewart and Jeff Chandler. *Director*: Delmer Davies.

Apache (1954). A tough, believable film based on the story of Massai, the last fighting Apache. Starring Burt Lancaster. *Director*: Robert Aldrich.

Stagecoach (1939). Against a background of one of Geronimo's outbreaks from the reservation, and with a tremendous sequence in which the Apaches attack the coach, this film was the first great Western. Starring John Wayne and many more. *Director*: John Ford.

Space only permits brief mentions of some others to watch out for: *The Searchers, Hombre, Butch Cassidy and the Sundance Kid* (despite the gags), *True Grit, The Shootist, The Big Sky, Run of the Arrow, Rio River, 3.10 to Yuma, The Big Country, A Man called Horse* (not for the squeamish), *Bad Day at Black Rock* (a modern Western), *How the West was Won*.

BOOKS

Fiction

It is safest to stick to a handful of reliable authors, the best of the moderns for the general reader who cares about the right atmosphere being Jack Schaefer and Dorothy M. Johnson. Zane Grey was the finest of the old generation of Western writers, while Owen Wister's *The Virginian* (1902) was the first classic. Also to be recommended are A. B. Guthrie's *The Way West* about the Oregon Trail, Elliott Arnold's *Blood Brother*, mentioned above, Paul Horgan's *A Distant Trumpet*, and Walter von Tilburg Clark's *The Ox-Bow Incident*.

Fact

The field is vast and many American titles are available in Britain or can be ordered. The University of Oklahoma Press has books on nearly every Indian tribe, while the Time-Life series on the Old West is a visual feast and many of the series have good texts. Here are a suggested basic six books to get:

The American Heritage Book of Indians (Eyre and Spottiswoode)
The Truth about Geronimo by Britton Davis (Yale)
The Banditti of the Plains by A. S. Mercer (University of Oklahoma Press)
Frontier Justice by Wayne Gard (University of Oklahoma Press)
A Tenderfoot in Colorado by R. B. Townshend (University of Oklahoma Press)
Six Years with the Texas Rangers by James Gillett (Yale)

PLACES TO VISIT

Few can afford a trip to the American West, but there is more to see in Britain than you might expect. **The American Museum at Claverton** near Bath has a number of displays about the West, including one on pioneers and how they crossed the Plains, and another on the Gold Rush, also one on cowboys. **Cowtown, U.S.A.** can be found at Great Yarmouth under the direction of Sheriff Danny Arnold, and this is a recreation that can be strongly recommended. Every gun used in the Wild West can be inspected in the **Tower of London.**

Among the many British museums that have Red Indian collections are the **Museum of Mankind** in London, the **City of Liverpool Museum,** the **City of Glasgow Corporation Art Gallery,** the **Ashburton Museum** at Ashburton in Devon, the **University Museum of Aberdeen** and the **University Museum of Archaeology and Ethnology** at Cambridge. Most wildlife parks have Western animals. At Camphill in County Tyrone, Ulster, an **Ulster-American Exposition and Folk Park** was opened in 1976, which has much to interest those interested in the buildings of the Old West.

For further information about the Wild West, there is the **English Westerners' Society,** the secretary of which can be contacted at 29 The Tinings, Monkton Park, Chippenham, Wiltshire.

Index

The numbers in **bold** refer to
illustrations and captions